big juniper house

National Park Service Archeological Series

*These publications are no longer available from the Superintendent of Documents, but may be ordered by title
(and parenthetical code number) by writing to: Clearinghouse, U.S. Department of Commerce, Springfield, Virginia 22151.
These reports are available in two forms: microfiche at 65¢ per document, or paper copy at $3.00 per volume, prepaid.

ARCHEOLOGICAL RESEARCH SERIES NUMBER SEVEN-C

Wetherill Mesa Excavations

big juniper house

Mesa Verde National Park — Colorado

by Jervis D. Swannack, Jr.

NATIONAL PARK SERVICE • U.S. DEPARTMENT OF THE INTERIOR
WASHINGTON 1969

U.S. DEPARTMENT OF THE INTERIOR
Walter J. Hickel, *Secretary*

This publication is one of a series of research studies devoted to specialized topics which have been explored in connection with the various areas in the National Park System. It is printed at the Government Printing Office and may be purchased from the Superintendent of Documents, Government Printing Office, Washington, D.C. 20402. **Price** $5.00

NATIONAL PARK SERVICE
George B. Hartzog, Jr., *Director*

LIBRARY OF CONGRESS CATALOG CARD NUMBER: 77—600350

foreword

From 1959 to 1963, the National Park Service, with generous support from the National Geographic Society, made a comprehensive study of the archeology and ecology of Wetherill Mesa, in Mesa Verde National Park. Wetherill Mesa is being developed so that increasing numbers of visitors will be able to observe the evolution of a prehistoric Indian culture over some 700 years, both here and in the nearby and more familiar section of the park known as Chapin Mesa.

This is the third monograph of the Wetherill Mesa Project. Big Juniper House, a small mesa-top ruin, is of interest chiefly as a manifestation of culture-in-transition during the 11th and 12th centuries. Additional reports in the series will deal with other Wetherill Mesa sites, as well as various aspects of the ecology and archeology of the area.

GEORGE B. HARTZOG, JR.
Director

acknowledgments

BIG JUNIPER HOUSE was excavated between May 14 and July 24, 1962, under my direction, acting under the general supervision of James A. Lancaster, archeologist at Mesa Verde National Park. The work crew consisted of J. Lester Goff and Horace A. Ruckel, foremen, and Victor Barney, Mark Hadley, Richard E. Lee, Kee Nez, Richard Parsons, Douglas H. Scovill, Michael Shaw, Donald E. Smith, Charlie R. Steen III, John W. Wade, and Paul Willie, laborers.

The field photographs were taken by Ruckel, Scovill, and myself. The laboratory photographs were taken by Fred E. Mang, Jr., project photographer, who developed and printed all the pictures. I owe Fred a special debt of gratitude for layout suggestions and other illustrative innovations.

Bill Wade and I drew the field maps. The final map of site locations on Wetherill Mesa (fig. 3) was done by Wade, with the other maps and plan layouts being completed for publication by George A. King, architect, of Durango, Colo.

Bone artifacts and unworked bone were examined by Lyndon L. Hargrave and Thomas W. Mathews, of the Southwest Archeological Center, Globe, Ariz. Hargrave identified the bird bones and Mathews identified the mammal bones.

Physical anthropological observations on the burials were made by Kenneth A. Bennett, University of Arizona. Human bone pathologies were identified by James S. Miles, M.D., of the University of Colorado Medical Center, Denver.

Thomas P. Harlan, of the Laboratory of Tree-Ring Research, University of Arizona, dated the wood and charcoal specimens recovered during the excavations. Paul S. Martin, of the Geochronology Laboratories, University of Arizona, supervised the identification of pollen grains extracted from the several soil profiles taken at Big Juniper House.

Stanley L. Welsh, Brigham Young University, identified the wild vegetal material, and Hugh C. Cutler, of the Missouri Botanical Garden, St. Louis, identified the charred corncobs and kernels.

Felix Mutschler, a geologist with the Kennecott Corporation, Durango, Colo., identified the material of the various stone artifacts, as a personal favor.

Richard P. Wheeler, laboratory supervisor of the project, and I analyzed jointly the stone artifacts, and Wheeler gave me advice in analyzing the bone artifacts. Douglas Osborne, supervisory archeologist of the project, studied the stone-chipping debris of Big Juniper House and the other sites excavated on Wetherill Mesa.

Many suggestions and ideas for this report were provided by other members of the project staff: George S. Cattanach, Jr., Charles L. Douglas, James A. Erdman, Alden C. Hayes, Robert F. Nichols, Carolyn M. Osborne, and Arthur H. Rohn. Bernard S. Katz, project editor, offered helpful suggestions in drafting the report. Al Lancaster contributed the knowledge of his long experience in Southwestern archeology during and after the excavation of Big Juniper House. To him I owe much of my understanding of Mesa Verde archeology.

My thanks go to the museum assistants who cleaned, cataloged, and mended the broken pots, and performed many of the technical and clerical chores that follow an archeological excavation. In particular, I would like to mention Pauline Goff, who helped me with the pottery analysis; Marilyn Colyer, who made the line drawings of the stone artifacts; and Jean Lee, who did most of the work of preparing the plates for reproduction.

Big Juniper House was also the subject of a thesis submitted in partial fulfillment of the requirements for an M.A. degree in anthropology at the University of Arizona. I am grateful to Raymond H. Thompson, Kenneth Hale, and Clara Lee Tanner, members of my thesis committee, for guidance and valuable advice.

References are made in this report to materials from a number of cliff and open sites on Wetherill Mesa which were excavated by the project and which will be reported on in due course. The cliff sites are Mug House (Arthur H. Rohn), Long House (George S. Cattanach, Jr., and others), Step House (Robert F. Nichols and others), and Site 1291 (Jervis D. Swannack, Jr.). The open sites include Badger House (Alden C. Hayes and James A. Lancaster), Two Raven House, Site 1230, Site 1253, and Site 1801 (Jervis D. Swannack, Jr.).

This publication is Contribution 34 of the Wetherill Mesa Project.

May 1966   *J. D. S., Jr.*

contents

tal

CHAPTER 1

the excavation and the environment

The archeological survey of Wetherill Mesa was in its final season. Canyon and cliff sites had been located and recorded, and a small crew continued the survey on the mesa top. On May 6, 1960, in a rather dense section of woodland south of Mug House, two house mounds were located and designated as Site 1595. Several large junipers grew on the mounds, the largest one—about 30 feet high and about 3 feet in diameter—being rooted in a kiva depression (later called Kiva B). Although this tree was felled (along with the others) in preparation for the excavation, it impressed itself on our minds. Subsequent reference to Site 1595 as "the big juniper site" took hold and led to our naming it Big Juniper House.

REASONS FOR EXCAVATION

The decision to excavate Big Juniper House was based on two objectives. One was to provide an interesting exhibit-in-place for visitors to Mesa Verde National Park; the other, to obtain information about an inadequately understood phase of occupation in the Mesa Verde region.

Before excavation, surface pottery and architectural features indicated a transitional phase from Pueblo II to Pueblo III. As excavation progressed, we saw that one of our obectives could not be realized—the site would not be suitable as an exhibit in the interpretive program. It had been occupied continuously for some 250 years, and building styles were not clearly differentiated stratigraphically. Some rooms even showed four different masonry styles and construction periods in a single wall. Moreover, the pueblo itself did not present a coherent, compact unit. "Horizontal stratigraphy" is harder to understand than vertical stratigraphy, and visitors with little time to spend at the ruin would be baffled rather than enlightened. In discussions between the park's interpretive staff and the project archeologists, it was decided the site should eventually be backfilled. (Badger House and Two Raven House, mesa-top ruins of Pueblo II and Pueblo

III, south of Big Juniper House, were picked as suitable for exhibit purposes.)

The withdrawal of interpretive interest permitted thorough excavation, usually impossible because of stabilization and exhibition requirements. Walls could be dismantled where and when needed; floors could be dug through; and backdirt could be piled wherever convenient. The work proceeded rapidly, and the second objective—to obtain information on the Pueblo II–III transition—was fulfilled.

LOCATION AND ENVIRONMENT

Mesa Verde National Park comprises about half of a large south-sloping tableland or mesa in southwestern Colorado (fig. 1). The mesa is demarcated on its north and west sides by a steep escarpment rising 1,000 to 2,000 feet above the surrounding country, and it is transected in its eastern and southern sections by the Mancos River Canyon. Headward-eroding streams have carved the tableland into northwest-southeast trending canyons creating many small mesas, one of which is called Wetherill Mesa (fig. 2). The name "Mesa Verde" (green table) derives from the perpetually green forest of pinyon and juniper that covers much of the tableland.

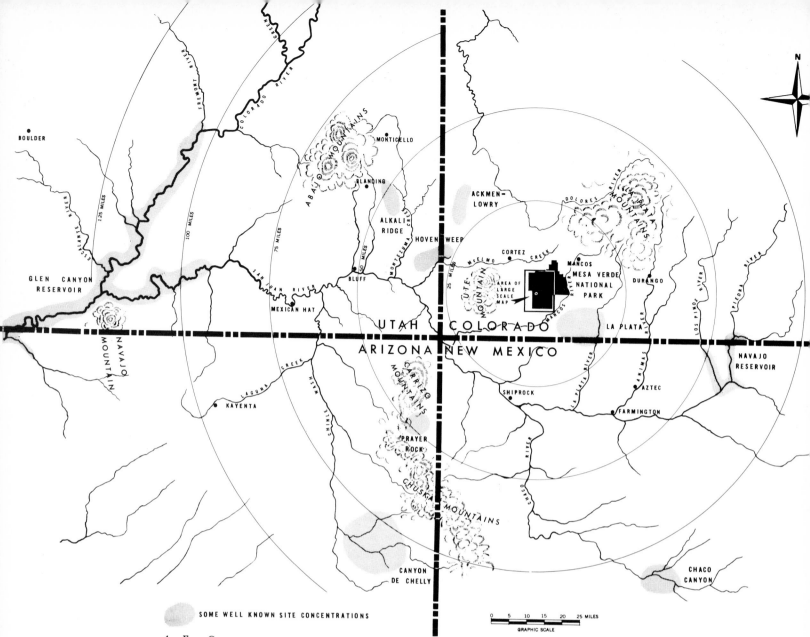

SOME WELL KNOWN SITE CONCENTRATIONS

0   5   10   15   20   25 MILES
GRAPHIC SCALE

1   *Four Corners area.*

The sedimentary rocks exposed in the area are primarily sandstones and shales, with intrusions of small igneous bodies and dikes (Wanek, 1959). The stratigraphic sequence runs from the Dakota sandstone (the oldest), through the Mancos shale, Point Lookout sandstone, and the Menefee formation, to the Cliff House sandstone (the youngest). Locally, the Cliff House sandstone is overlain by small bodies of cemented gravels which are probably derived from the La Plata and San Juan Mountains.

Big Juniper House is on the west side of Wetherill Mesa, approximately 380 yards due east of Rock Canyon and Jug House (Site 1233), and about 820 yards due west of Long Canyon (fig. 3). The altitude at the site is approximately 7,220 feet.

The site is on a low, east-west ridge that slopes in all directions. Figure 4 gives an idea of the general terrain. The greatest slope is to the south, following the inclination of Wetherill Mesa. The site faces toward the south, with the rooms on the north followed by the kivas and the trash mound.

The undisturbed soil of the site is a red loess, the bottom of which was not encountered in excavations as deep as 10 feet. The loose forest humus on the surface rarely exceeded one-half foot in depth.

In general, the climate of the Mesa Verde region is characterized by low humidity and wide, diurnal temperature ranges. Average annual precepitation over a 38-year period, beginning in 1923, was 18 inches. Two wet periods occur during the year: in late winter, with moisture primarily from snowfall, and in late summer, with moisture usually from afternoon thunderstorms. The wettest months are February and August, the driest are June and November. In 1962, when Big Juniper House was excavated, Mesa Verde National Park recorded its driest summer, with precipitation of 0.74 inches for June, July, and August. The average precipitation during these months in the 38-year period of record was 4.4 inches.

The warmest month is July, with a mean temperature of 72°F., and the maximum recorded temperature of 102°F. The coldest month is January, with a mean temperature of 29°F. The lowest recorded temperature at Mesa Verde, −20°F., occurred in January 1963.

The area of Big Juniper House is a woodland of pinyon and Utah juniper, with an understory consisting chiefly of mutton grass. Big sagebrush and black sagebrush grew on the house and trash mounds. These shrubs are commonly found on the disturbed soil of other prehistoric sites at Mesa Verde (Erdman, MS.).

Common animals observed in the area are the coyote, mule deer, bobcat, gray fox, Nuttall's cottontail, rock squirrel, Colorado chipmunk, brush mouse, deer mouse, and pinyon mouse. Badger, porcupine, and red fox are seen occasionally.

Birds observed today with varying frequencies are the scrub jay, pinyon jay, common raven, common crow, hairy woodpecker, and red-tailed hawk. Brief appearances are made by the broad-tailed hummingbird, plain titmouse, robin, western bluebird, and chipping sparrow.

Turkeys, probably domesticated or kept in captivity by the prehistoric inhabitants, became extinct in the Mesa Verde historically and were re-introduced in the park in 1944, 1955, and 1957. They are now most common near the park's staff residential areas where food is relatively abundant. However, they have also been observed in other parts of the park. They are native to, and numerous in, areas not far from Mesa Verde, such as the White Mountains of Arizona and the Sangre de Cristo Mountains in New Mexico.

EXCAVATION PROCEDURE

Excavation began by stripping soil from the center of the West House Mound to the outside until walls were found. As rooms were outlined, they were numbered consecutively (fig. 5). Levels within rooms were arbitrary or, in some cases, were by the natural stratigraphy. Artifacts from the floor or, if no floor was encountered, from the level corresponding to the base of the walls were always bagged and cataloged separately from artifacts recovered in the fill. Artifacts from floor features, subfloor tests, and subfloor features were also bagged and cataloged separately.

Areas adjacent to the rooms and kivas were stripped down in an effort to discover occupation surfaces and extramural features. Artifacts from these features were bagged and cataloged separately from those of general proveniences within the areas.

Kivas A and B, marked by circular depressions, were trenched to find the walls and then stripped down by artificial and natural levels. Kiva C was located by a soil auger, trenched, and then stripped. All rooms and kivas that were completely excavated were also tested below floor levels—usually by two trenches at right angles to each other—and dug to sterile native soil. Subfloor features were completely excavated. Artifacts from the kiva floors, floor features, and subfloor features and tests were handled in the same manner as those from rooms.

2 *Aerial view of Wetherill Mesa.*

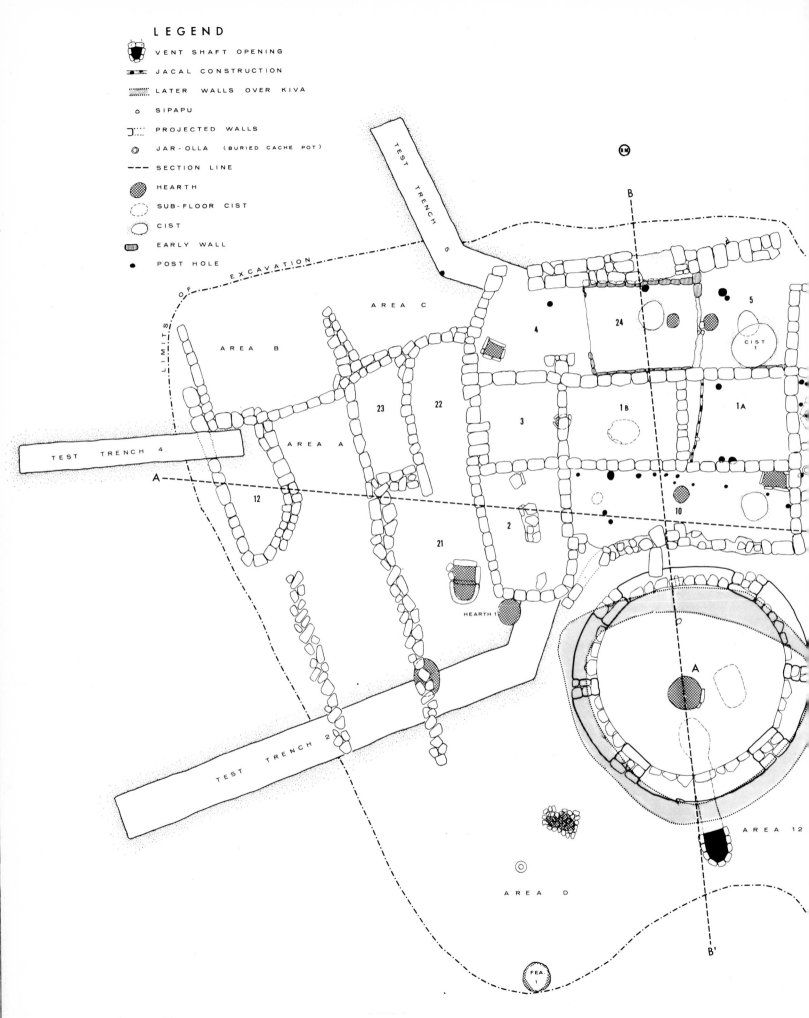

LEGEND

VENT SHAFT OPENING

JACAL CONSTRUCTION

LATER WALLS OVER KIVA

SIPAPU

PROJECTED WALLS

JAR-OLLA (BURIED CACHE POT)

SECTION LINE

HEARTH

SUB-FLOOR CIST

CIST

EARLY WALL

POST HOLE

LIMITS OF EXCAVATION

TEST TRENCH 5

TEST TRENCH 4

TEST TRENCH 2

AREA B

AREA C

AREA A

AREA D

AREA 12

4

24

5

CIST 1

23

22

3

1B

1A

12

2

21

10

HEARTH 1

A

FEA 1

B

B'

A

24

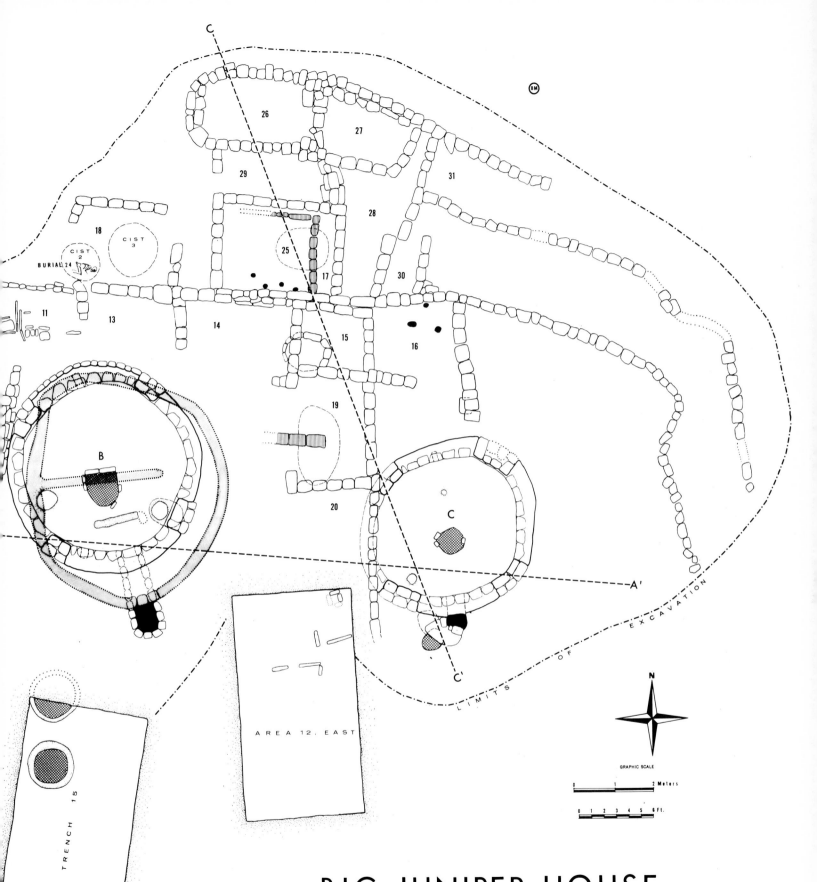

5 BIG JUNIPER HOUSE

SITE 1595

WETHERILL MESA ARCHEOLOGICAL PROJECT

MESA VERDE NATIONAL PARK

COLORADO

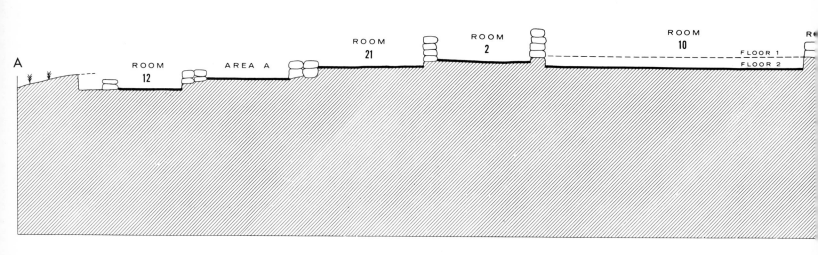

A

ROOM
12

AREA A

ROOM
21

ROOM
2

ROOM
10

FLOOR 1

FLOOR 2

R

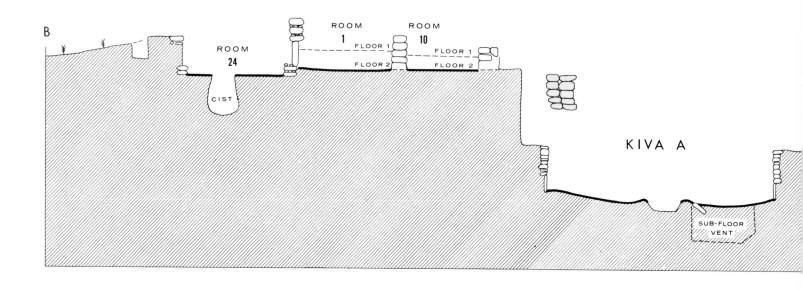

B

ROOM
24

CIST

ROOM
1

FLOOR 1

FLOOR 2

ROOM
10

FLOOR 1

FLOOR 2

KIVA A

SUB-FLOOR
VENT

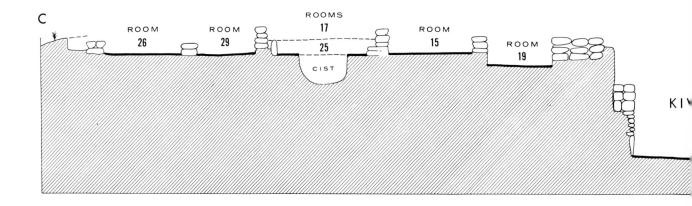

C

ROOM
26

ROOM
29

ROOMS
17

25

CIST

ROOM
15

ROOM
19

KIV

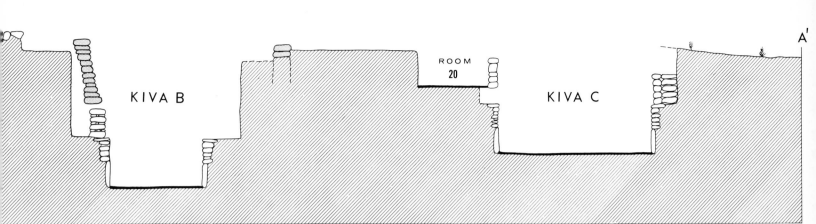

KIVA B

ROOM
20

KIVA C

A'

B'

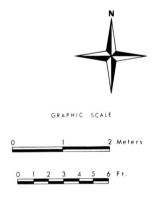

N

GRAPHIC SCALE

0   1   2 Meters

0 1 2 3 4 5 6 Ft.

━━━━ FLOOR LINE

C'

CIST

6 BIG JUNIPER HOUSE

SITE 1595

WETHERILL MESA ARCHEOLOGICAL PROJECT

MESA VERDE NATIONAL PARK

COLORADO

Component	Associated Features
E ca. A.D. 1150	Later walls over Kivas A and B. Probably the compound wall north of Rooms 24 and 5.
D ca. A.D. 1080–1100 to 1130	Main occupation of the site. Late occupation of Kiva A. Kivas B and C. Upper fills and walls of Rooms 1a, 1b, 10. Rooms 2, 3, 4, 6, 7, 8, 9, 11, 13, 14, 15, 16, 17, 19, 20. Probably Rooms 21, 22, 23, 26, 27, 28, 29, 30; also Areas A, B, C, D.
C ca. A.D. 1050–80	Lower fill and Floor 2 of Rooms 1a, 1b, 10. Hearth below shared wall of Rooms 1b and 3. Posts below floor of Rooms 7 and 8. Possibly Room 12. Clay-lined firepit under slab hearth and probably Hearth 1 in Room 21. Room 25. Probably Area 12 and Test Trench 15, and the two firepits in Test Trench 15. Firepit under retaining wall in Test Trench 2. Posts under floor of Room 16. Feature 1. Cist to south of Kiva C. Probably early occupation of Kiva A.
B Ca. A.D. 900–1000	Room 5. Subfloor hearth in Room 6. Subfloor cist in Room 7. Cists 2 and 3; cist under wall of Room 25. Subfloor cist in Room 19. Possibly firepit cut by cist south of Kiva C.
A Within time range of Component B, but possibly earlier part of that range.	This is a possible earlier component based on the floor level of Room 24. It may also be part of Component B. Room 24. Sub-Floor 2 cist in Room 1b. Sub-Floor 2 cist in Room 10. Post below Room 21. Post in Test Trench 5. Possibly Pit 1 in the South Trash Mound next to Test Trench 1. It is possible that this pit is earlier than Component A.

Most of the unexcavated parts of the East House Mound probably belong to Component D. The East Trash Mound is also primarily of this component. The South Trash Mound was undoubtedly used during all the components.

In addition to the five construction components, there appeared to be at least two occupational units of kivas and related rooms. The more clearly delineated unit includes Kiva A; Rooms 1a, 1b, 2, 3, 4, 6, 7, 8, 9, 10, 11, and probably Rooms 21–23; and Area D. This unit is composed of several functional categories: living rooms, mealing or work rooms, storage rooms, and courtyard-outdoor work areas. Units are primarily defined on the basis of proximity to kivas, wall junctures indicating times of construction, and contiguity of rooms and areas.

The second unit is Kiva B; Rooms 13–15, 19, 20; and possibly Rooms 17 and 18. There does not seem to be a comparable occupation unit related to Kiva C.

These units will be described under the individual rooms and kivas.

Twenty rooms, or areas numbered as rooms, and three kivas were completely excavated and tested below floor level. In addition, 11 rooms or areas were outlined in the East House Mound, and miscellaneous walls, hearths, and cists scattered around the house area were excavated. The South Trash Mound was almost completely excavated by a series of parallel trenches. Only one trench

was dug in the East Trash Mound, which turned out to be a shallow deposit over a natural hillock, yielding little material of importance.

The architectural terms used in this report are defined as follows:

Coursed masonry—masonry in which the stones are laid in layers.

Slab wall—a wall in which the stones are set on edge.

Jacal wall—a wall consisting of a framework of poles or small posts and interwoven twigs or smaller poles covered with adobe; often called "wattle and daub." Jacal walls at Big Juniper House are termed so only by inference. The remains of such walls at the site consist of burned stubs of the vertical members with burned clay between, the rest of the wall having disintegrated.

Simple wall—a wall of coursed masonry, one building stone in width; these walls are sometimes called "single-coursed walls"—a misleading term, since courses refer to layers and not to widths.

Double wall—a wall composed of two simple walls—each wall laid adjacent to but independent of the other.

Compound wall—a wall of coursed masonry, two or more building stones in width; some or all of the stones are exposed on only one face of the wall.

Rubble wall—a wall composed of unworked stones with no apparent coursing or facing.

Scabbled masonry—building stones that have initial shaping by edge-spalling; stones are blocky in appearance.

Chipped-edge masonry—masonry in which the stones are shaped by bifacial chipping or spalling; sides and ends of the stones have usually been worked to thin, sinuous edges.

Finished masonry—masonry in which the initial shaping is by one or both of the above methods, followed by pecking or grinding, usually confined to the faces.

ROOMS AND AREAS

It is difficult to say with any certainty what specific function a room or area served. In fact, as will be seen in the following discussion, some "rooms" might be considered areas. I could not determine what rooms were used only for sleeping, so I have called most rooms "living rooms." This indicates a general-purpose function. A living room could, and probably did, serve at one time or another as a place to sleep, to work, or to store things. On the other hand, when I refer to a storage room or workroom, this is because there appears to be a more definite reason to do so, such as the small size of the room or the presence of mealing bins or of storage jars in the floor.

Room 1a

Dimensions. About 8.5 feet long east-west and about 6.5 feet wide north-south; lower level (Floor 2) was approximately 2.7 feet below present ground surface (figs. 7 and 8). Part of the north wall was 0.2 to 0.4 feet above ground surface; part of the south wall was at surface.

Walls. Masonry walls all belong to the Component D building period. The west wall was constructed later than the other walls. East wall abuts north wall, south wall abuts east wall, west wall abuts north and south walls. Rooms 1a and 1b were possibly a single room at

7 *Room 1a, Floor 2.*

one time. The jacal wall on the west side is in Floor 2 and extends under the south wall; it belongs to the Component C building period. The top 1.6 feet of the north wall is finished masonry and is banded with small tubular spalls arranged in even layers between the larger building stones (fig. 9). This masonry was originally chipped-edge masonry that was later finished on the faces by pecking. The south wall is chipped-edge masonry and some finished masonry of the same type as in the north wall. The east wall is chipped-edge masonry.

8 *Plan and sections of Rooms 1a and 1b.*

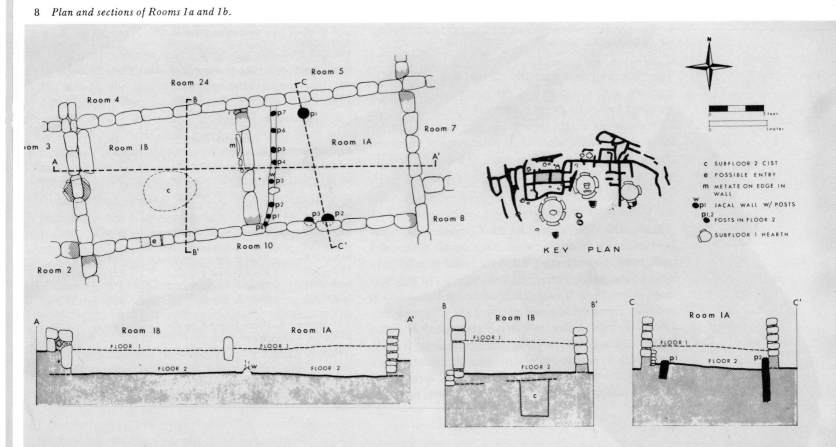

Although there are only three dates from the subfloor cist—two from *in situ* posts that were probably wall supports for the slab lining—they appear to be close to the construction date of the cist. The two dates for the subfloor surface above the cist are also fairly close together and are well within the range of dates listed for Rooms 1a, 1b, and 10.

Remarks. Because of its small size and the cache pots in the floor, Room 7 was probably a storage room—one of a unit composed of Rooms 6, 7, and 8, and possibly also Room 11, a work and mealing room that will be discussed later. The subfloor level represents Component C and is probably part of the same structure described for Floor 2 of Room 1a. The subfloor cist is on the same level as the subfloor hearth in Room 6 and probably belongs to Component B. Three components are thus represented in Room 7.

Room 8

Dimensions. About 5.1 feet long east-west and 2.8 to 3.5 feet wide north-south (figs. 17 and 18). The floor is 0.7 to 1.7 feet below present ground surface.

Walls. All are simple walls primarily of chipped-edge masonry. North and south walls abut the west wall and are bonded to the east wall. Maximum standing heights above floor area: north wall, 2 feet; west and south walls, 1.6 feet; east wall, 0.8 foot.

The east wall extends about 1.3 feet below the floor, other walls rest on the floor level except for that part of the west wall shared with Room 1a, which extends below the floor level of Room 8.

Entry. None indicated.

Floor. Hard-packed use surface resting on approximately 1.7 feet of fill above sterile soil. The floor is slightly basin-shaped and about on the same level as the Room 7 floor. Beneath the floor was an occupation surface of Component C equivalent to Floor 2 in Rooms 1a and 10.

Artifacts on floor. Buried in the western side of the floor was a Mancos Black-on-white olla (fig. 57a), with its opening at floor level. In the southwestern corner of the floor was a Type 1C mano (fig. 100d), half buried in the floor.

Near the center of the room were the burned remains of Burial 6 (fig. 169). This was a secondary burial resting on the floor. Associated with it were burned fragments of rush matting and an unburned late Mancos Black-on-white bowl (fig. 56c). Also in probable as-

17 *Plan and sections of Rooms 6, 7, and 8.*

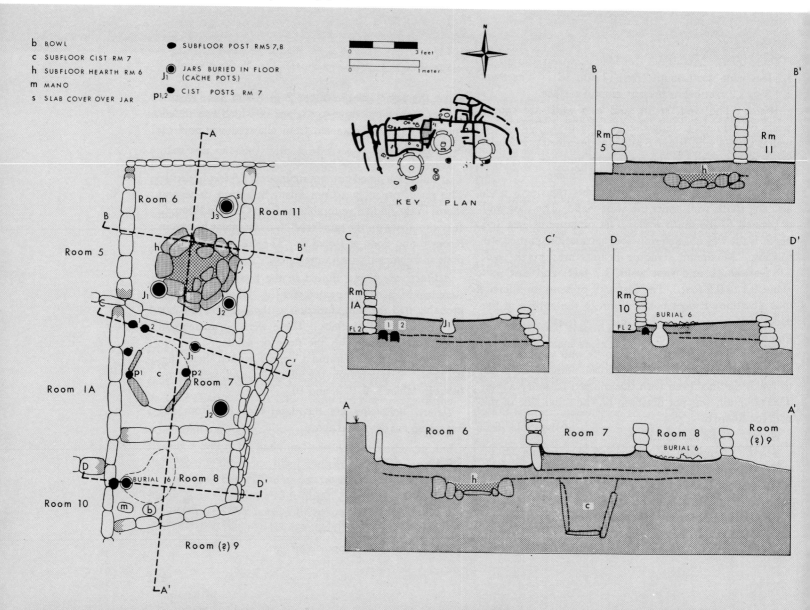

sociation were a Type 8 worked sherd (fig. 86, center) and an unclassified black-on-white sherd. Artifacts in the room fill and subfloor fill are listed in tables 3, 8, and 9.

Dates. The following dates were derived from beneath the floor—one from an *in situ* post in the Component C surface and one from charcoal fragments below the Component C occupation:

Specimen	Provenience	Dates, A.D.	
		Inside	Outside
MV–1695	Post beneath west wall........	873	1000vv
MV–1694	Subfloor, 3.4 ft. below present.. surface.	925	990vv

(NOTE: See table 17 in appendix for key.)

As in Room 7, these two dates show a slight separation between the Component C occupation and the Component B occupation. They are much closer, however, than those from Room 7, which cluster in two groups.

Remarks. Room 8 was probably a storage room during the Component D occupation and was used after its abandonment for the interment of Burial 6. Wall junctures of Rooms 6, 7, and 8 suggest that Room 6 was originally constructed as part of the unit of Rooms 1a, 1b, and 10. Sometime later, Rooms 7 and 8 were added as storage rooms for the unit.

Room 9

Dimensions. About 4 feet long north-south and 2 feet wide east-west (fig. 5). Not a definite room. The floor (or an occupation surface?) is about 1.5 to 2 feet below present surface.

Walls. The north and west walls are shared with Rooms 8 and 10, respectively. They are simple walls of primarily chipped-edge masonry. The east wall is a probable compound wall two courses high, mostly of scabbled masonry. The north wall abuts the west wall and the east wall abuts the north wall. No south wall was located. Walls averaged about 1 to 1.3 feet above the floor and probably rested on it.

Entry. The missing south wall may have contained an entry.

Floor. A use-packed surface resting on approximately 1 foot of disturbed fill. No subfloor features.

Artifacts. None were found on the floor or in the subfloor fill. Artifacts from the room fill are listed in tables 3, 6, and 9. A small mortar (fig. 102, left) was discovered on the west wall.

Dates. No absolute dates. Probably a Component D feature.

18 *Room 7 (upper left) and Room 8 (foreground). Cache pots in floors of both rooms.*

Remarks. Room 9 most likely served as a storage room and was probably part of the storage unit of Rooms 6, 7, and 8.

Room 10

Dimensions. About 17.6 feet long east-west and 5 to 5.8 feet wide north-south (figs. 19 and 20). Floor 2 level is 2.1 to 2.6 feet below present ground surface.

Walls. The north, east, and west walls are simple walls. The south wall is rather indefinite and irregular, and may have been a simple wall. It had no apparent coursing or facing. The east and west walls are composed primarily of chipped-edge masonry, the north wall of chipped-edge stone and some pecked-faced masonry, and the south wall (those stones remaining) is primarily of chipped-edge masonry. All these walls belong to Component D and rest on 0.4 to 1 foot of fill above Floor 2, the Component C level.

The west wall abuts the north wall, the north wall abuts the east wall, and it is likely that the south wall also abuts the east wall. The southwest corner is too fragmentary to determine the wall juncture.

Entry. Possible entry in the north wall from Room 1b.

Floor. Floor 1 was not definitely located but is probably level with the top of the slab-lined hearth in the northeastern corner of the room, about 1.4 feet below the top of the east wall. This is at about the same depth as the presumed Floor 1 of Rooms 1a and 1b.

Floor 2 was clearly delimited by a fire-hardened surface in which several postholes were excavated and two burned posts were imbedded. These and burned roofing beams supplied dates. There is a firepit in the north-center part of the room. Floor 2 is part of the same surface represented by Floor 2 in Rooms 1a and 1b and the subfloor posts in Rooms 7 and 8.

About 0.5 and 0.6 foot below Floor 2 were signs of another occupation surface and two cists. They are probably features of Component A or B, as is the sub-Floor 2 cist in Room 1b.

Artifacts on floor. No definite association of artifacts with either Floor 1 or 2 or the sub-Floor 2 occupation surface. Sherds listed in table 3 from Room 10 hearth are from the Floor 1 hearth fill and include McElmo Black-on-white sherds, indicating a definitely later occupation than the Floor 2 level. Artifacts listed from Upper Fill are from Room 10 fill above the level of the slab-lined hearth. Lower Fill artifacts come from the room fill below this level to just above Floor 2, and Floor 2 fill artifacts come from about 0.3 to 0.5 foot above the floor to the floor. Some artifacts were found in the fill of sub-Floor 2, Cist 1; none were found in sub-Floor 2, Cist 2.

19 *Room 10, Floor 2, in center. In left corner (northeast) is hearth, a Floor 1 feature. Burned roofing logs rest on Floor 2. To left of Room 10 are Room 1a (top) and Room 1b; to right is Kiva A.*

outdo...
is a lo...

Sim...
interre...
by int...
and d...
House...
alterat...

Room

Dim...
widest,
larly sl...
The fl...

Wall...
about ...
posed ...
about v...

The
walls a...
curve a...
out a d...
about (...
west wa...

Entry...

Floor...
ing dire...
observe...

Artifa...
the floo...
fill and ...

Dates...
Compo...

Rema...
of the la...
city of r...
area sug...
donment...
quent co...

Room 1...

Dimen...
(fig. 5).
of both ...
were mis...
present d...
3.5 feet ...
the same...

Walls.
masonry.
have bee...
wall appe...
north wa...
However,
wall of R...
juncture i...

Entry.

Floor.

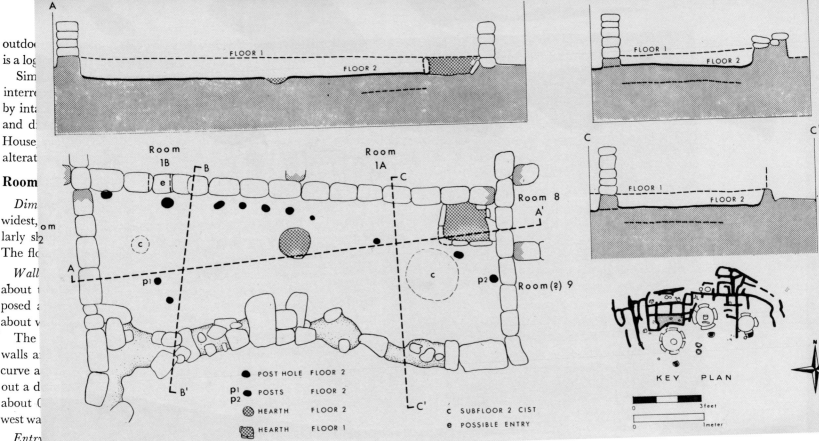

20 *Plan and sections of Room 10.*

The artifacts are listed in tables 3, 9, and 10.

A restorable Mesa Verde Corrugated jar (fig. 44, left) was found in the upper fill of Room 10, near the east wall close to the slab-lined hearth, and was probably on Floor 1.

Dates. All dates listed in table 2 are from juniper charcoal from Floor 2 (Component C). One date came from sub-Floor 2, Cist 1 fill, and probably represents fill from the Floor 2 occupation.

TABLE 2. — TREE-RING DATES FROM ROOM 10, BIG JUNIPER HOUSE

Specimen [1]	Provenience	Dates, A.D.[2] Inside	Dates, A.D.[2] Outside
MV–1680.....	Fill, resting on Floor 2....	893	1041vv
MV–1668.....	Fill, resting on Floor 2....	921	1039vv
MV–1687.....	Floor 2, Post 2..........	812p	1028+vv
MV–1673.....	Fill, resting on Floor 2....	933p	1028vv
MV–1670.....	Fill, resting on Floor 2....	925	1027vv
MV–1735.....	Sub-Floor 2, Cist 1, fill..	911	1024vv
MV–1667.....	Fill, resting on Floor 2....	931p	1022+vv
MV–1678.....	Fill, resting on Floor 2....	910	1018vv
MV–1685.....	Fill, resting on Floor 2....	800	1008+vv
MV–1660.....	Fill, resting on Floor 2....	893±	1007vv
MV–1686.....	Floor 2, Post 1..........	855±	993vv
MV–1677.....	Fill, resting on Floor 2....	924	992vv
MV–1666.....	Fill, resting on Floor 2....	897p	985r
MV–1672.....	Fill, resting on Floor 2....	859p	947vv
MV–1679.....	Fill, resting on Floor 2....	814	886vv

[1] Specimen numbers assigned by the Laboratory of Tree-Ring Research, University of Arizona.

[2] Key to symbols: p—pith ring present; v—outside shows erosion, outermost ring variable around circumference; vv—outside shows extreme erosion, outermost rings variable; r—outer ring constant over significant portion of circumference.

The dates from Room 10 are within the range of those from Room 1a. In the 985r date, the "r" indicates that the outside ring is constant around the circumference, and the date is therefore a probable cutting date. This specimen may represent a re-used beam. The fact that the 985 date is close to the Component B dates from Rooms 7 and 8 strongly suggests that this specimen was originally used as a Component B construction item and then later taken for the Component C building or buildings, represented by Floor 2 of Rooms 1a, 1b, and 10. All the other dates have inconsistent outer rings and probably do not represent cutting dates.

Remarks. The Component D walls of Room 10 enclose the largest area of any of the surface rooms at the site. However, the placement of the slab-lined hearth suggests a courtyard or working area rather than an enclosed room. The south wall is possibly a retaining wall rather than a room wall, as there does not seem to be any apparent coursing or alinement with the other walls of the room.

The Floor 2 occupation is part of Component C, previously described for Rooms 1a and 1b.

If, during the Component D occupation, Room 10 was an outdoor working area, we have several different types of rooms combined in a relatively coherent functional unit. Rooms 1a, 1b, possibly Room 2, and Room 3 were living rooms; Room 11 was a work or mealing room; Rooms 6, 7, 8, and 9 were storage rooms; Room 10 was a courtyard-outdoor work area at the south; and the Room 4 area, extending west over Rooms 24 and 5, was an analogous courtyard-outdoor work area at the north side of the rooms.

41

commonly found in Pueblo III kivas, although it is a rare trait in that period. However, more sites, and many more kivas, of Pueblo III than of earlier periods have been excavated in the Mesa Verde area. As a result, the subfloor ventilator data may be "overweighted" for comparative purposes. Remodeling of subfloor ventilators to floor-level ventilators, as in Kiva A, is quite typical of Pueblo III kivas.

It has also been suggested that four-pilastered kivas did not have cribbed roofs, but rather followed the old roofing pattern of the four-post kivas or "proto-kivas" and pithouses of earlier times (Lancaster and Pinkley, 1954, pp. 55–56). The roofs in these are assumed to consist of four horizontal beams placed on the roof supports. In the case of Kiva A, the primary beams rested upon the four masonry pilasters over which smaller poles spanned the rectangular space to form the top of the roof. Other small construction members were placed from the four primary beams to the top of the earthen kiva walls to form the sides of the roof. Shakes, bark, reed, or other material, and a coat of adobe finished off the roof. It is not a hard and fast rule, but this generally appears to be the pattern. It is almost a certainty that six- and eight-pilaster kivas, primarily confined to Pueblo III, had cribbed roofs and therefore they reflect a basic change in roof construction.

It is probable, then, that Kiva A underwent a major remodeling that included a change from a subfloor to floor-level ventilator, and a four-pilaster "old" kiva roof design to a six-pilaster, cribbed-roof of "modern" design. The pit next to the hearth was probably filled and plastered over at this time, too.

The question remains as to why Kiva A was remodeled. If the kiva had been in good condition there would have been little reason to tear down the roof, install two new pilasters, and build a new roof. If Kiva A was extensively changed, as has been suggested, it must have fallen into a state of disrepair and perhaps the roof had already collapsed. Although there is little evidence at Big Juniper House to suggest abandonment of the site between Components C and D, there may have been a time when Kiva A was not in use. Perhaps there was insufficient manpower to keep it in good repair. If, as seems likely, the population increased at the beginning of the Component D occupation, with new styles in architecture including most of the masonry rooms at the site, the reoccupation of an older kiva with appropriate changes in its design would probably have been easier than building a completely new one. It is also probable that sometime after Component D began, Kivas B and C were constructed to accommodate other groups.

From its relationship to the surface rooms at Big Juniper House, Kiva A may be considered an integral part of an occupation unit. This has been mentioned in my remarks on Rooms 10 and 11. During the Component D occupation, the roof of Kiva A was probably part of an outdoor courtyard or work surface that included Room 10 and Area D, and possibly Rooms 21 and 22. It was probably the focus of religious and social activities for the people of the occupation unit as well.

Later, Kiva A was used as a trash dump and a wall was built over it. The purpose of this wall is a mystery, but it appears to be a feature restricted to kivas. One other example is Kiva B, and similar later walls over kivas were found at Two Raven House and at Sites 1230 and 1253.

Kiva B

Dimensions. About 13 feet in diameter, varying between 12.8 and 13.2 feet (figs. 25 and 26). Floor is approximately 8.3 feet below present ground surface. The inside dimensions of the later wall constructed over Kiva B are 17.1 feet long north-south and 14.2 feet wide east-west.

Banquette. Kiva B followed the same style of banquette facing as in Kiva A—a base of slabs with intermixed and overlying coursed masonry (fig. 27). Sherds and sandstone spalls were also used for chinking as in Kiva A. Several of the stones in the banquette face were dressed by pecked facing, a situation that did not occur in Kiva A. The remainder of the stones were primarily scabbled, with a few chipped-edge. The banquette averaged about 2.8 feet above the floor; it was plastered on top with about 0.2 foot of adobe mud. There was also some plaster remaining on the banquette face, but not enough to determine the presence of multiple coats. The width of the banquette averaged about 1.5 feet, with a range of 1 to 2 feet.

Liner above banquette. Kiva B was the only kiva at Big Juniper House with a liner above the banquette, a common feature of Pueblo III kivas in the Mesa Verde area. The liner was built only on the north part of the banquette, between the second and third pilasters, and was similar in style to the banquette face, having a slab base topped by coursed masonry of small stones (fig. 28). However, smaller stones were used in the liner than on the banquette. It was probably about the same height, 2.3 feet, as the second pilaster. The remainder of the wall above the banquette was the dirt wall of the original excavation and was probably plastered.

Later wall over kiva. The later wall built over Kiva B was constructed on fill at the level of the tops of the pilasters, and extended down lower on the west side to slightly above the level of the banquette. The later wall over Kiva B was similar in most respects to the wall over Kiva A; the one difference is the existence of a cross wall or partitioning wall that was bonded to the west part of the later wall and extended east (fig. 29). The height of the later wall ranged from 3 to 4.1 feet and averaged about 3.5 feet. The highest point was at the western side near the area of the cross wall. Portions of the later wall were exposed at the present surface. As in the Kiva A later wall, approximately 25 percent of the building stone was pecked faced, the rest scabbled or chipped-edge. We found no occupation surface to indicate whether there was a room or structure inside the later wall and the cross wall. The later wall was most clearly defined on the north and west sides where it was carefully stepped back from bottom to top, to a maximum displacement of 1.9 feet on the north side.

Niches. There were two niches. One was in the usual

place on the kiva axis in the northern portion of the banquette face (fig. 28). It was about a 0.3-foot-square opening with the top inner edge 0.4 foot below the top of the banquette. It extended into the banquette 1.3 feet. The other niche was in the southern banquette face about 0.6 foot east of the first pilaster. Its dimensions were 0.45 foot wide, 0.2 foot high, and 0.7 foot deep. Nothing was found in either niche.

The north niche was difficult to find, having been filled and plastered over. The other niche was probably open.

Ventilator. The ventilator was a floor-level type, probably originally masonry lined throughout, and the shaft was built of both slabs and coursed masonry. Slabs, probably supported by wooden lintels, made up the tunnel roof, and the sides of the tunnel were coursed masonry. The tunnel floor was native earth.

Pilasters. Kiva B had four pilasters, all flaring from front to rear and set back from the edge of the banquette 0.15 foot. They ranged in height above the banquette from 1.6 feet (fourth pilaster) to 2.3 feet (second pilaster). The other two pilasters were nearly 2 feet high. The fourth had partially fallen, and it is probable that it, too, was about 2 feet high when the kiva was used.

The pilasters had pecked-face stones with the corners nicely squared. They were decorated with bands of small sandstone spall- and sherd-chinking between the courses of the larger stones.

Floor. The basin-shaped floor was formed by about 0.3 foot of adobe applied on the sterile earth.

The hearth was a D-shaped pit, 0.7 feet in maximum depth, with several small sandstone slabs and rocks mudded into its sides. It was filled with fine white ash and contained no artifacts.

No sipapu was found.

Two cists were in the floor: Cist 1 below the fourth pilaster, and Cist 2 between the first and second pilasters. Both had been filled with trash and plastered even with the floor before the kiva was abandoned.

Cist 1 has a flat floor and deeply undercut sides, extending about 1.1 feet under the banquette on the east. Its depth is approximately 2.6 feet. In the cist fill we found eight sherds (table 3), two Type 1A manos, one Type 2 hammerstone (table 9), and a miniature ladle (fig. 90). We also found an unfired teardrop-shaped clay pendant (fig. 96, left) and a number of unworked bones of turkey, black-tailed jackrabbit, deer, and unidentified mammals (tables 12 and 13).

Cist 2 had straight sides and a flat floor, and was approximately 0.8 feet deep. Four sherds were the only artifacts found in the fill (table 3).

The deflector was indicated by a mud line of a different color from the surrounding floor (fig. 25). It is assumed the deflector was a short jacal wall—a type of deflector found occasionally in Mesa Verde kivas. It was situated about 1 foot from the south edge of the hearth and about 2.1 feet from the ventilator opening. The deflector was about 3.4 feet long and 0.6 foot wide, with a possible extension on the east side that curved south.

Entry. No entry was indicated, but it is assumed that there was a hatchway in the roof above the hearth.

Other features. None.

Artifacts on floor. The plan and photograph of Kiva B show the location of artifacts found on the floor (figs. 25 and 26). Pottery consisted of a restorable Mesa Verde Corrugated jar (Pot 1), close to the east side of the hearth (fig. 44b); a partially restorable Mancos Corrugated jar (Pot 2), southwest of the hearth; the base of a black-on-white jar (Pot 3), north of the Mesa Verde Corrugated jar; a partially restorable Mancos Corrugated jar (Pot 4), close to Pot 3; a partially restorable Mummy Lake Gray jar (Pot 5), north of the ventilator opening (fig. 36); a Mancos Black-on-white bowl (fig. 56f), in the same area as Pot 5; and a Mancos Black-on-white jar, also in the same general area as Pot 5. Sherds of the last two were found, respectively, on the floor of Kiva C and on the floor of Kiva A.

Stone artifacts included a Type 2 hammerstone, next to Pot 1; a Type 2 hammerstone, next to Pot 2; a Type 1 hammerstone, northeast of Cist 2; a pitted hammerstone (fig. 116f), over the east side of Cist 2; a Type 1A mano, in the Pot 2 area; a Type 1A mano, close to the north banquette face between pilaster 2 and the north banquette face niche; a full-grooved, unfinished ax (fig. 118a), over the west side of Cist 2; a bird-shaped concretion (fig. 141, left), possibly a pot support west of the hearth; a Type 1 unspecialized milling stone, to the north of the hearth; a Type 4 unspecialized milling stone, over the southeast side of Cist 2, next to the pitted hammerstone; an unmodified pebble showing possible slight use as a polishing stone, east of the pitted hammerstone and Cist 2; and a large, unmodified flake, over the north side Cist 2. Also on the floor below the third pilaster were two skeletons, one of rabbit and one of kangaroo rat. A Type 1 unspecialized milling stone was just under the floor and below the second pilaster.

One of the most interesting finds at the site was an apparent cache of eight mammal bone awls and a mammal bone scraper (fig. 149, ch. 5). These were found 3 feet east of the ventilator, in the fill next to the southern portion of the banquette. They had probably fallen from the banquette.

The following artifacts were on the banquette: a large Mancos Black-on-white jar sherd (fig. 62 1); a Type 3 deer bone awl and a Type 2 hammerstone, on the western portion of the banquette; a combination-grooved abrader and three utilized flakes, on the north part of the banquette; and a roughly rounded slab fragment, on the south banquette. A whole Mancos Black-on-white miniature ladle (fig. 90), found in the fill near the second pilaster, might have fallen there from the banquette. Pottery sherds taken from the fill just above the banquette are listed in table 3 as Kiva B, Banquette Fill.

Fill. There was no discernible stratigraphy in the fill. The kiva was excavated in artificial levels to the floor, and no significant change was noted in the artifact types recovered. In the lower fill and floor fill we found a restorable McElmo Black-on-white bowl with a corrugated exterior (fig. 73a). Stone and bone artifacts, sherds and worked sherds found in Kiva B fill are listed in tables 3, 6, 8, 9, and 10. The quantity of artifacts

27   *Detail of Kiva B banquette face.*   28   *Detail of north section of banquette face with niche, Kiva B.*

29   *Later walls over Kiva B on north (top of picture) and west sides, and part of cross wall in the center.*

them but not integrated into the room block. Kiva C presents a somewhat anomalous situation that will be discussed later.

Kiva B, from its probable dating, was a Component D occupation feature. The later wall over Kiva B is considered a Component E feature, probably constructed after 1130 but before 1150.

As discussed previously under Rooms 14, 19, and 20, Kiva B was likely a focal point for an occupation unit consisting of Rooms 13, 14, 15, 19, and 20. The roof of this kiva probably served as a courtyard-working area for this assumed occupation unit. Other rooms behind the main north wall of Rooms 13 to 15 may also have been part of this unit, but their relationship to Kiva B is not as clear as the above rooms.

Kiva C

Dimensions. Kiva C is less circular than Kivas A and B. The dimensions are approximately 10.4 feet wide north-south and 11.5 feet long east-west (figs. 30 and 31). The floor lies from 6.2 to 7.3 feet below the present surface.

Banquette. The same style of banquette facing that was observed in the other kivas—a base of slabs intermixed and overlain with coursed masonry (fig. 32)—was present in Kiva C. No pecked-face rocks were observed in the banquette face or the pilasters. The stones were primarily scabbled, with a few being chipped-edge.

The banquette was 3 feet above the floor and its width averaged 1.5 feet, with a range of 1.2 to 2 feet. The banquette is wider between the third and fourth pilasters than between the first and fourth and between the second and third.

There were traces of at least three layers of plaster on the banquette face, to a maximum thickness of 0.1 foot. A relatively thick layer of yellow, sandy plaster was overlain by two thin coats of brown plaster.

There was no liner above the banquette and the native earth of the kiva excavation served as the wall above it. Originally, this may have been plastered.

No later wall was built over the kiva as in Kivas A and B. The east wall of Room 20 skirted the kiva on the west side, but it was probably constructed over part of the kiva roof and consequently fell in after the roof collapsed, as shown in figure 30.

Niche. Kiva C had one niche, 0.3 foot square, which extended about 0.7 foot into the north portion of the banquette face on the kiva axis. The inside top of the niche was 0.6 foot below the top of the banquette. In the niche were a Type 2B worked sherd, a Mancos Black-on-white jar sherd, and two unmodified cores.

Ventilator. The ventilator had a floor-level tunnel and probably a masonry-lined vertical shaft. It appears that the shaft was constructed through an old cist which, in turn, cut through an older firepit. Because of the soft fill in the ventilator area, most of the stones that lined the shaft had collapsed and little remained of the original shaft lining. The ventilator tunnel did not appear to have been lined behind the banquette face. The native earth provided the walls, ceiling, and floor of the tunnel.

Pilasters. All of the Kiva C pilasters flared from front to rear and all were set back from the edge of the banquette an average of 0.1 foot. They were unlike Kiva B pilasters, however, for they were wider and lacked pecked-face masonry. In fact, the fourth pilaster was so wide that it had to be shaped inward to conform to the curve of the banquette. The masonry of the pilasters was scabbled and chinked with small stones or spalls. Kiva C also differed from the other two kivas in the absence of sherd-chinking in the pilasters and the banquette face.

Floor. The floor in Kiva C was basin-shaped and silghtly lower in its northern part. Approximately 0.2 foot of adobe applied to the sterile earth formed the floor. There were no subfloor features.

The hearth was a circular pit about 2 feet in diameter and 0.6 foot deep, slightly deeper on the south side. It had three sandstone concretions or "pot supports" mudded in the sides (fig. 140), and was filled with ash.

A sipapu was located on the kiva axis about midway between the hearth and the north banquette face. The cylindrical hole measured 0.4 foot in diameter and 0.7 foot in depth.

A small cist covered by a sandstone slab (fig. 136b) was next to the banquette, beneath the first pilaster. It is a cylindrical hole 0.8 foot in diameter and 0.85 foot deep. Nothing was found inside it.

No deflector was found. Three irregularly shaped slabs lay on the floor between the ventilator and the hearth, but their size and arrangement precluded their use as either ventilator covers or deflectors. Probably they were part of the collapsed roof.

Entry. As in the other kivas, no evidence of an entry was found. It is assumed that it was a hatch directly above the hearth.

Other features. None.

Artifacts on floor. The plan of Kiva C (fig. 31) shows the position of the various stone, bone, and pottery artifacts in place on the floor and on the banquette.

Pottery on the floor included: a Mancos Black-on-white bowl (fig. 56f), on the west side of the kiva near the cist; a partially restorable Mancos Black-on-white jar (fig. 57d), in the same area; a Type 10 worked sherd (fig. 83a), on the east side of the floor; and a Type 7 worked sherd (fig. 83c), on the south side, to the west of the ventilator. Sherds of the Mancos Black-on-white bowl were also found on the floor of Kiva B.

Stone artifacts on the floor were: a Type 2A mano (fig. 101b) on the east side of the floor below pilaster 4; a Type 1 unspecialized milling stone with a red paint stain on one grinding surface (fig. 103d) on the west side of the floor; a Type 2 unspecialized milling stone (fig. 104b) next to the west side of the hearth; a Type 4 unspecialized milling stone (fig. 104h) to the east of the sipapu; a "jar lid" (fig. 136g) to the northeast of the sipapu, which may have been used to cover this feature; the sandstone slab covering the cist, as mentioned previously; a handstone (fig. 105e) on the southeast portion of the floor beneath the fourth pilaster; three Type 2 hammer-

ceramics

Approximately 13,600 sherds and 56 complete or partially restorable vessels were recovered during the excavation of Big Juniper House. All the pottery was examined macroscopically to determine rim shape, neck form, surface treatment, slip, paint type, and decorative style. Representative sherds were then selected for microscopic examination of temper and, in some cases, the presence or absence of a slip.

Worked sherds, miniature vessels, pipes, and other ceramic objects are described in this chapter under separate headings. They are not included in the sherd counts of the types discussed immediately below.

Pottery manufactured in the Mesa Verde area in prehistoric times is assigned to two wares: Mesa Verde Gray Ware and Mesa Verde White Ware. They are separated on the basis of surface treatment—the plain and textured utility or culinary pottery is assigned to Mesa Verde Gray Ware, and the black-on-white painted pottery is designated as Mesa Verde White Ware.

Mesa Verde Gray Ware includes the types called Chapin Gray, Moccasin Gray, Mancos Gray, Mummy Lake Gray, Mancos Corrugated, and Mesa Verde Corrugated. Mesa Verde White Ware includes Chapin Black-on-white, Piedra Black-on-white, Cortez Black-on-white, Mancos Black-on-white, McElmo Black-on-white, and Mesa Verde Black-on-white. All but Mesa Verde Black-on-white were found at Big Juniper House.

A third ware, San Juan Red Ware, is encountered in small quantities at sites in the park. In this report, the ware is divided into two types: Abajo Red-on-orange and Bluff-La Plata Black-on-red. Very few of these sherds were found in relation to the number of black-on-white or gray sherds, and their distinctive paste sets them apart from the usual pottery found at Big Juniper House. We do not know if red ware was locally produced or not. The period of occupation at Big Juniper House was late enough so that very little red ware of the Alkali Ridge series would be expected to survive in use. The contemporary Tusayan Black-on-red and Citadel Polychrome types, to the west, were evidently far enough removed in space so that very little of these would be found in the Mesa Verde region.

MESA VERDE GRAY WARE

Plain Gray Body Sherds

No attempt was made, other than in a trial run, to type the 612 plain gray body sherds. Body and base sherds of the plain gray pottery made in the Mesa Verde region are indistinguishable from the body sherds from plain portions of textured vessels. Surface treatment of plain vessels and plain sections of textured vessels appear to have changed very little through time.

Probably many of these sherds are from Mancos Gray or Mummy Lake Gray vessels rather than earlier plain gray types such as Chapin Gray or Moccasin Gray. The major use of these latter types was prior to the occupation of Big Juniper House. Very few black-on-white types of this early period are represented at the site, adding more evidence that the plain gray body sherds came from types later than Chapin Gray or Moccasin Gray.

The sherds, primarily from jars, usually have scraped or smoothed surfaces, and some display a light polish on the exterior. They are unslipped and range from light to dark gray.

Approximately 90 percent of the sherds examined microscopically have crushed rock temper. Temper in several sherds is a combination of rock and sherd, and in a few others it is sand or crushed sandstone.

Ten body sherds can be considered as local gray pottery with decorations on the exterior due to experimentation or method of construction. Four are punctated and five are incised (fig. 33). There is a possibility that these nine sherds are from trade vessels. They are similar to O'Leary Tooled and Honani Tooled, both of which

36 *Mummy Lake Gray jar; height, 24 cm.*

Mummy Lake Gray

One restorable jar (fig. 36) and 39 rim sherds (figs. 37 and 38) of Mummy Lake Gray pottery were found at Big Juniper House. This site was one of several excavated by members of the Wetherill Mesa Project that provided information for the recently described pottery type (Rohn and Swannack, 1965).

Mummy Lake Gray jars are plain over the entire surface, except where an unindented coil or fillet forms the rim. Occasionally, parts of the surface show traces of the original coiling. Body shape and rim form generally parallel those of Mancos Corrugated, although Mummy Lake Gray vessels are comparatively small.

The characteristic rim fillet of Mummy Lake Gray was almost obliterated on the restorable jar that was found. Its dimensions are 24 cm. high, 20.8 cm. in maximum diameter, and about 17 cm. in orifice diameter. Its capacity, measured with vermiculite is 4.8 liters (a compar-

37 *Mummy Lake Gray rim sherds. The rims are straight to slightly flaring except g, which is sharply everted.*

Corrugated Body Sherds

No attempt was made to separate the 4,771 indented-corrugated body sherds into Mancos Corrugated and Mesa Verde Corrugated types. As a group, Mesa Verde Corrugated shows less variation in surface treatment than Mancos Corrugated, but there is no sharp division between them. Most of these body sherds may be identified as Mancos Corrugated because of the preponderance of rim sherds and restorable vessels of this type.

One hundred and fifty-two sherds are patterned-corrugated (fig. 39), a more common trait in Mancos Corrugated than in Mesa Verde Corrugated. The only form represented by the corrugated body sherds are jars. Pitchers have been found in other sites.

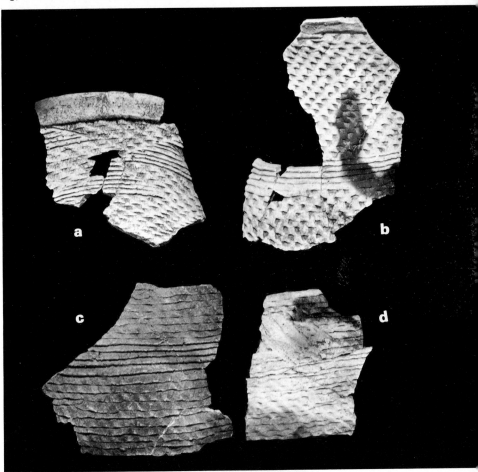

39 *Mancos Corrugated sherds showing typical forms of patterning; rims sherds, a, b, e, and body sherds, c, d.*

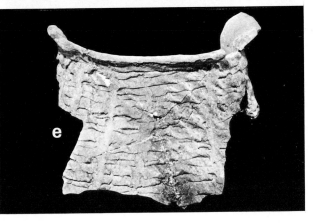

38 *Mummy Lake Gray rim sherds with exterior and interior views of sherd with mineral-painted "H" on interior.*

atively large Mummy Lake Gray vessel). All of the rim sherds are from jars, although pitchers are quite common vessel forms. Tempering material is primarily crushed rock. A few sherds are tempered with a combination of crushed rock and sherds and one or two sherds are tempered with sand or crushed sandstone.

One of the sherds has a mineral-painted "H" on the interior, just below the rim (fig. 38). This figure is similar to the simple designs painted on the interior of several Mancos Corrugated rim sherds.

Mummy Lake Gray was made from about A.D. 950 to 1200, but its period of abundance was from about 1000 to 1150 (Rohn and Swannack, 1965). The one restorable vessel at Big Juniper House was found on the floor of Kiva B along with Pueblo III vessels—a Mesa Verde Corrugated jar and a McElmo Black-on-white bowl. The jar probably dates from about 1100 to 1130 on the basis of dated charcoal from the kiva.

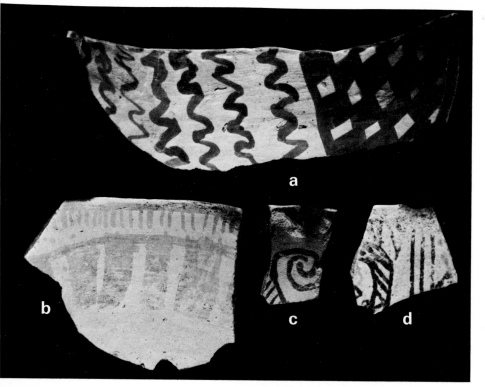

49 *Cortez Black-on-white bowl sherds with combination designs.*

50 *Cortez Black-on-white jar sherd with a combination design. Present maximum length about 22 cm.*

51 *Cortez Black-on-white sherds with combination designs.*

52 *Cortez Black-on-white sherds with combination designs.*

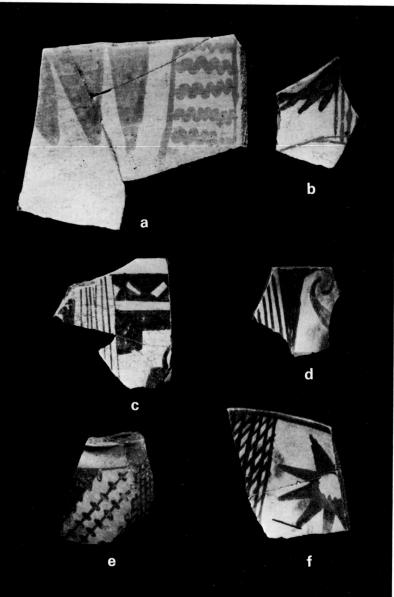

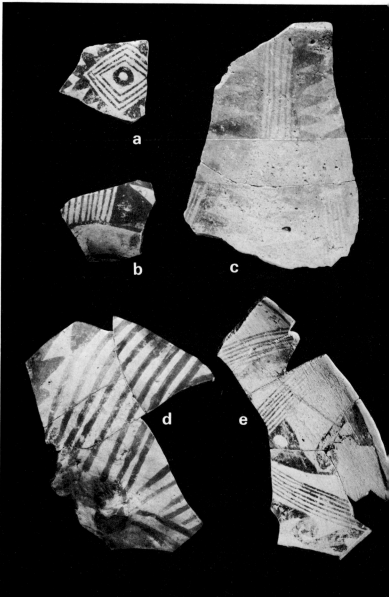

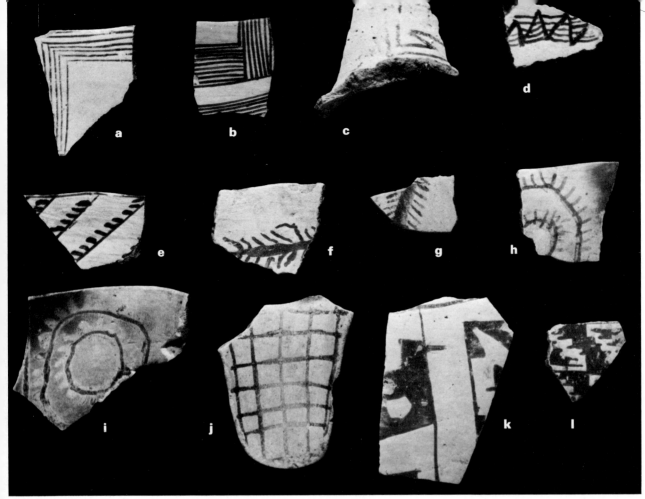

53　Cortez Black-on-white sherds with various designs: narrow line, a–d; ticked line, e–g; ticked circle, h, i; cross hatch, j; and stepped figure, k, l.

54　Cortez Black-on-white sherds with various designs: triangle and ticked/triangle, a–h; squiggle hatch, i, j; and squiggle line, k–p.

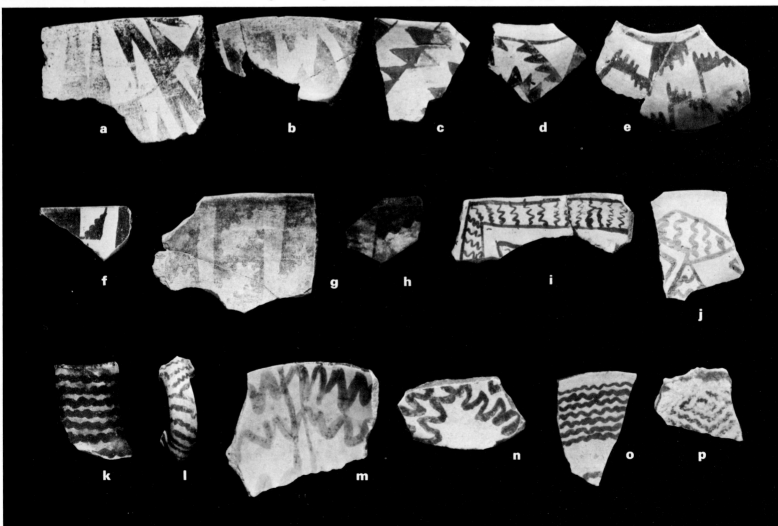

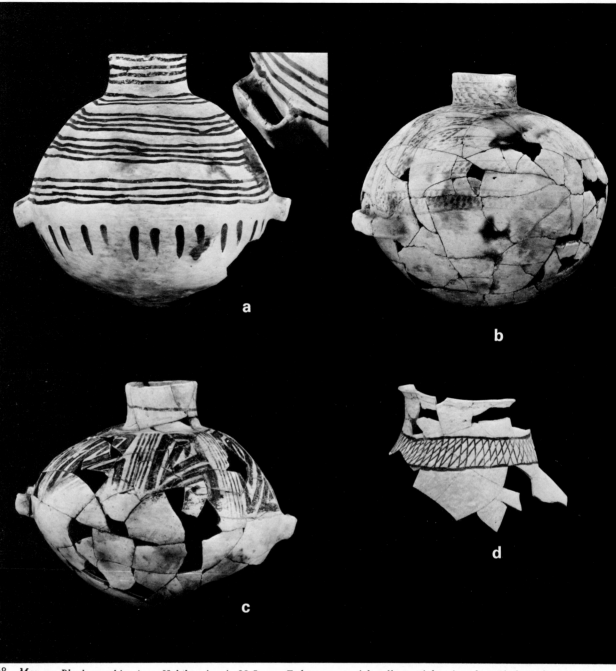

58   *Mancos Black-on-white jars. Height of a is 33.5 cm. Enlargement of handle to right of a shows indentation.*

59   *Mancos Black-on-white pitchers. Present height of a is 13.1 cm. Height of b is 16.1 cm. (c and d, same scale).*

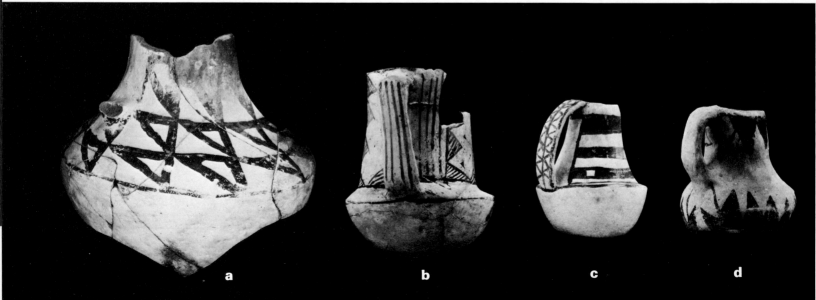

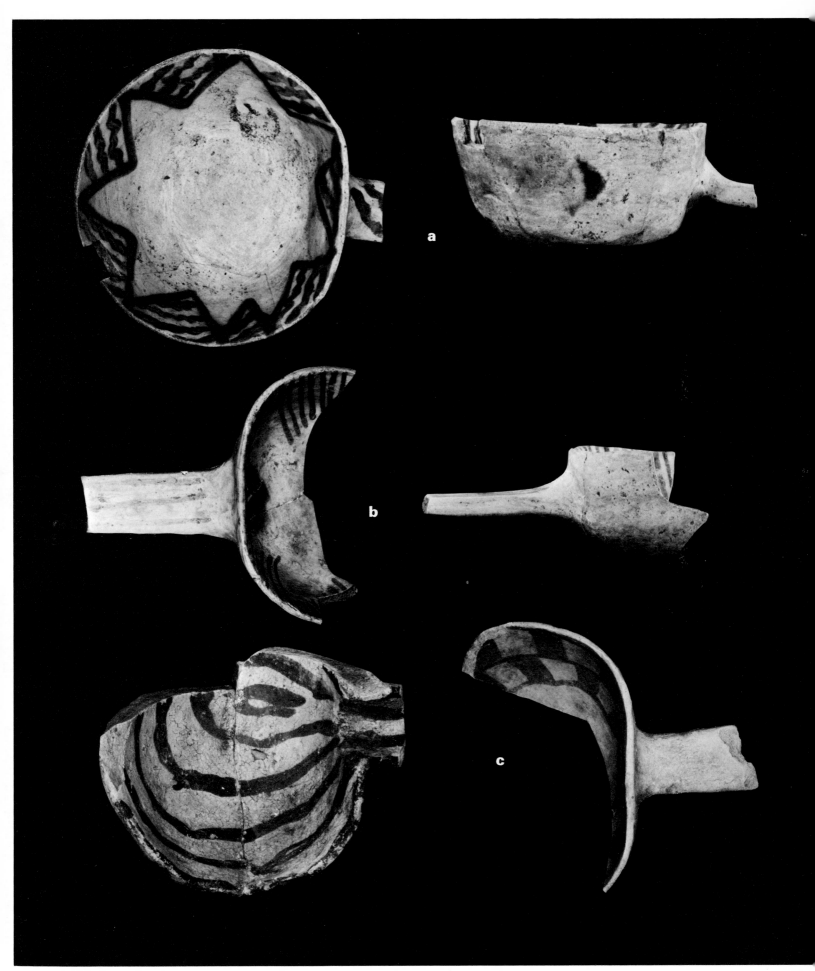

60   *Mancos Black-on-white ladles. Length of a is 12.7 cm.; b, 11.5 cm.; c, 8.0 cm.; and d, 11.7 cm.*

Checkerboard designs occur most frequently in band layouts, but triangles, simple lines often with pendent triangles, and other design styles are also used. Bands are never framed by lines as in McElmo Black-on-white or Mesa Verde Black-on-white. Figure 61 shows typical layouts of this type.

Although all of the design elements used on Cortez Black-on-white pottery also appear on Mancos Black-on-white, the way they are employed and the popularity of certain styles enable us to distinguish between the two. In Cortez, combinations of design elements and motifs are the most popular form of decoration; in Mancos, decorative elements and motifs are usually not combined. Combination designs account for only 5.6 percent of the various design styles employed on Mancos Black-on-white (fig. 62; table 5).

The most popular decoration on Mancos Black-on-white is a diagonal, straight-line hachure used as a filler between parallel lines which frequently form triangular or rectilinear frets (fig. 63). This style did not occur on Cortez Black-on-white sherds from this site as a single design, but did occur (in small numbers) in combination with other motifs. Diagonal, straight-line hatching combined with other motifs can be seen in the illustrations mentioned above.

Approximately 20 percent of all the Mancos Black-on-white sherds have the broad-line design style, which is almost nonexistent in Cortez Black-on-white sherds. The broad lines are usually arranged in triangular or rectilinear frets (fig. 64).

Triangles are probably used most frequently in the design pattern. They occur as solid triangles or as dots, broad and narrow lines, checkerboard, and hatching arranged to form triangles (fig. 65).

Other elements such as dots, squiggle hatch, cross hatch, checkerboard, and narrow lines are fairly common on Mancos Black-on-white (figs. 66–69).

Exterior decoration on bowls and ladles is more usual on Mancos Black-on-white than on Cortez Black-on-white and also shows more variety. Various arrangements of simple lines predominate, as well as designs not found on Cortez Black-on-white such as concentric circles and crosses (fig. 70).

Zoomorphic and geometric figures occur occasionally on Mancos Black-on-white bowl and ladle interiors (fig. 71), but they did not become popular until later, in Mesa Verde Black-on-white.

Rim decoration differs slightly from that of Cortez Black-on-white. One of the major differences is in the increased frequency of ticked rims—from 0.5 percent in Cortez Black-on-white to 3.1 percent of the Mancos Black-on-white—and a corresponding decrease in solidly painted rims in Mancos as opposed to Cortez. Dot ticking is predominant, but several sherds showed diagonal slashes on the rim tops.

Interiors of bowls and ladles and exteriors of jars and pitchers are usually slipped and polished. Crackling of the slip is also common. Exteriors of bowls and ladles are also usually slipped and polished, but less frequently than the interiors. Jar and pitcher interiors are slipped

TABLE 5.—PERCENTAGES OF DESIGN STYLES, CARBON PAINT, AND RIM DECORATION ON MANCOS BLACK–ON–WHITE SHERDS, BIG JUNIPER HOUSE

Design styles		Percent of style to total Mancos B/W sherds	Percent of carbon paint to sherds in the style	Percent of mineral paint to sherds in the style	Percent of plain rims to rims in the style	Percent of rims painted solid to rims in the style	Percent of ticked rims to rims in the style	Percent of indeterminate rims to rims in the style
Combination		5.6	.2	99.8	24.2	62.9	1.6	11.3
Checkerboard		8.2	4.3	95.7	17.7	55.6	6.4	20.2
Broad-line		20.19	7.2	92.8	24.5	47.3	4.4	23.9
Narrow-line		9.2	6.6	93.4	20.0	55.8	....	24.3
Triangle		14.9	6.7	93.3	33.1	47.4	1.9	17.5
Ticked triangle		.1	....	100	100	....	....	....
Squiggle hatch		5.3	....	100	14.7	64.7	....	20.6
Straight-line hatch		30.8	5.4	94.6	20.5	60.6	2.9	16.0
Cross hatch		3.8	3.4	96.7	15.7	74.5	2.0	7.8
Dots		3.8	5.1	94.9	38.9	22.2	16.7	22.2
Scroll		.1	100	....	....	....	....	100
Ticked line		.1	....	100	....	50	....	50
Step figure		.6	....	100	25.0	50	....	25.0
Ticked circle		.1	....	100	....	100	....	....
Overall percentages		100	5.4	94.6	22.9	54.9	3.1	18.7

a b c

d e f

g i j

h

k l m

just below the rim in rare instances. Color of the slipped surfaces is most often creamy white, less frequently slate gray. Unslipped surfaces usually have a grayish cast.

A sample of 160 Mancos Black-on-white sherds was examined microscopically, and 75 sherds had rock temper (about 46.9 percent), 27 sherd temper (about 16.9 percent), 48 sherd and rock temper (about 30 percent), 4 rock and sand temper (about 2.5 percent), 3 sand temper (about 1.9 percent), and another 3 sherds had sand and sherd temper.

These results disagree with Abel's (1955, Ware 12A, Type 5) statement that the only temper used in Mancos Black-on-white was crushed sherds. The number of variations in temper in these "good" Mancos Black-on-white sherds shows that temper is not a reliable criterion for pottery classification.

Generally, Mancos Black-on-white vessel shapes continue to be the same as those of Cortez Black-on-white. Bowls are steep-sided, approaching the vertical, but one restored bowl (fig. 57e) has exaggerated outsloping walls. Bowl bases generally are slightly rounded to flat; however, two bowls have indented bases, a characteristic usually confined to the black-on-white jars (fig. 57e and f). Several bowls, as in Cortez Black-on-white, have handles and lugs (fig. 72a–c).

65 *Mancos Black-on-white sherds with triangle designs.*

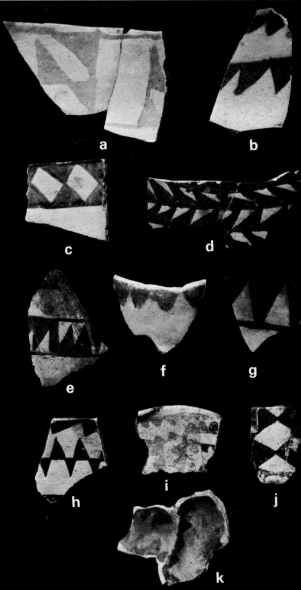

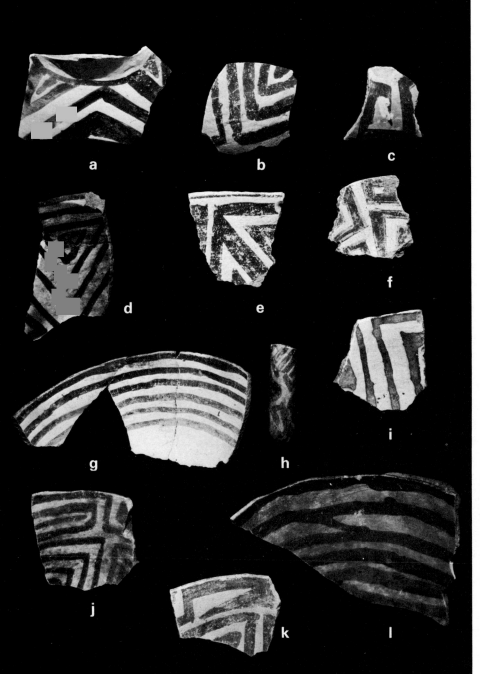

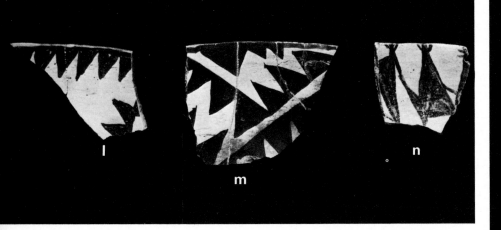

64 *Mancos Black-on-white sherds with broad-line designs.*

65 *Mancos Black-on-white sherds with triangle designs. Sherds l–n are bowl rims.*

66 *Mancos Black-on-white sherds with dot designs.*

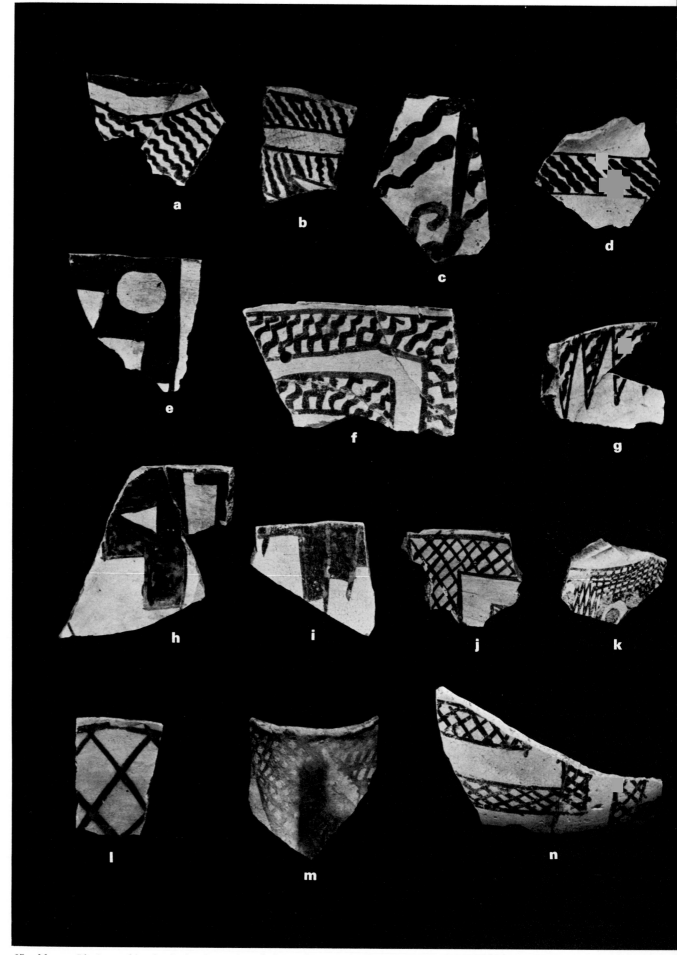

67 *Mancos Black-on-white sherds showing various design styles:* squiggle hatch, *a–d, f, g;* stepped figure, *e, h, i; and cross hatch, j–n.*

Mancos Black-on-white jars usually have globular bodies with short, cylindrical necks. One has a corrugated neck (fig. 58b). The jars, or ollas, generally have opposed lateral strap handles often indented in the middle (fig. 58a–c) or, occasionally, coil handles placed at the greatest diameter of the jar and just under the painted design (fig. 72d). Bases have a shallow kickup or indentation. One partially restored rim neck and shoulder (fig. 58d), with rim fillet and slightly flaring rim, resembles Mancos Corrugated and Mummy Lake Gray jars.

Mancos Black-on-white pitchers are characterized by truncated, cone-shaped necks, meeting the body either at sharp or gently curving angles. Strap handles are common and are placed parallel or slightly diagonal to the long axis, beginning at the rim or just below and usually ending at some point on the angle where the neck and body meet. Bases are indented.

Ladles are straight-sided and tend to have flatter bases than bowls. Forms are the same as Cortez, but the scoop type or half-gourd ladle was definitely less popular than the bowl-and-handle variety. Tubular handles occur more frequently than on Cortez Black-on-white ladles, but the commonest handles are solid and flat, oblong, or round in cross section. They are usually placed about midway between the rim and base, but one ladle (fig. 70f) has a handle that projects directly from the base.

Other forms of vessels occurring in the Mancos Black-on-white collection from Big Juniper House are plates, miniatures, and a bird effigy vessel (fig. 66b).

McElmo Black-on-white

This pottery type has long presented one of the more perplexing problems in Mesa Verde archeology. Controversy has ranged (and raged!) all the way from describing its characteristics and determining its associations, to questioning its validity as a type. I regard McElmo Black-on-white as a valid type, and in the chapters on architecture and stone artifacts I discuss cultural manifestations indicative of the period during which this type occurs. In the final chapter, I attempt to bring these manifestations together and draw some conclusions regarding the last stage of occupation at Big Juniper House—the transition from Pueblo II to Pueblo III.

Three restorable vessels (fig. 73) and 127 sherds (figs. 74 and 75) are identified as McElmo Black-on-white, the latest type of Mesa Verde White Ware found at the site. The quantity of McElmo Black-on-white sherds is small compared to that of Mancos Black-on-white and Cortez Black-on-white. The terminal occupation of Big Juniper House—during late Pueblo II and early Pueblo III, prior to A.D. 1150—was the most extensive. The scarcity of McElmo Black-on-white was thus not the result of few people living at the site, but rather because this pottery had just begun to be made at this time.

Findings at Fewkes' Unit Pueblo (O'Bryan, 1950, pp. 137–140) and at Sites 1230 and 1801 indicate that McElmo was probably the dominant decorated type at Mesa Verde from about 1150 to 1200, after which time Mesa Verde Black-on-white was the potters' choice.

68 *Mancos Black-on-white sherds with checkerboard designs.*

91

82 *Type 6 worked sherds, disks, often chipped around perimeter, some with grinding over chipping.*

84 *Type 7 worked sherds. At left, top and bottom views of solid, flat ladle handle; at right, part of ladle fashioned into possible pendant.*

83 *Type 7 worked sherds, derived from ladles, with grinding usually on broken section of handle, b–e; and Type 10 worked sherd, miscellaneous category, a.*

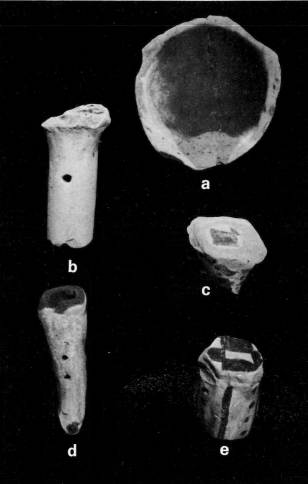

around the perimeter and sometimes ground over the chipping (fig. 82). These forms occur widely in the Southwest, but their function is not known.

An unusual category of worked sherds, designated Type 7, is represented by nine ladle sherds, with grinding usually on broken sections (figs. 83b–e, and 84). One section, ground smooth at both ends and with a small groove engraved around the circumference at one end, may have been a pendant (fig. 84, right). A possible use of worked tubular handles has been suggested by an artifact that Carolyn Osborne, who studied various museum collections for the project, observed at the University Museum, University of Pennsylvania. The object, originally from the McLoyd and Graham collection from Utah, is a piercer or dagger, consisting of a wooden pile and a tubular ladle handle as the grip (fig. 85). Our tubular ladle sherds may have had the same use.

Two bases from Mancos Black-on-white bowls and one plain base from a black-on-white jar classified as Type 8, were ground on the edges to form plates (fig. 86). None of them are whole. The worked jar base had fugitive red pigment over the entire inside surface and may have served as a paint palette. These sherds may also have been used as *pukis*, or platforms for rotating vessels during their construction (Guthe, 1925).

Three complete or fragmentary bases of corrugated jars, shaped into shallow bowls or possible *pukis*, are designated Type 9 (fig. 87). Two were chipped and slightly ground on the perimeter, but the third was chipped only on the edge.

Three sherds that do not fit into the other categories are classified as Type 10. The sherd illustrated (fig. 83a)

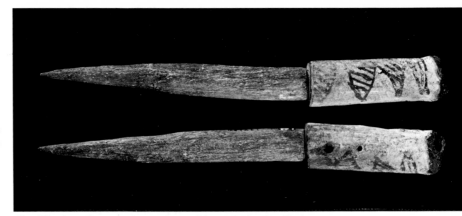

85 *Wooden piercer or dagger inserted into tubular handle (two views), indicating possible use of Type 7 worked sherds. Overall length about 25 cm.; handle only, about 9 cm. (Photo courtesy The University Museum, University of Pennsylvania.)*

is the indented base of a black-on-white jar. It is well ground on the exterior bordering the kickup, and the broken edge was chipped and lightly ground. It resembles a miniature bowl. The other two sherds are from a Cortez Black-on-white jar and from a black-on-white jar or pitcher. The Cortez sherd shows wear on

87 *Type 9 worked sherds, jar sherds worked into bowls; interiors at left, exteriors at right. Top sherd, 22 cm. in diameter; bottom sherd, 24.8 cm. in longest dimension.*

86 *Type 8 worked sherds, formed into plates.*

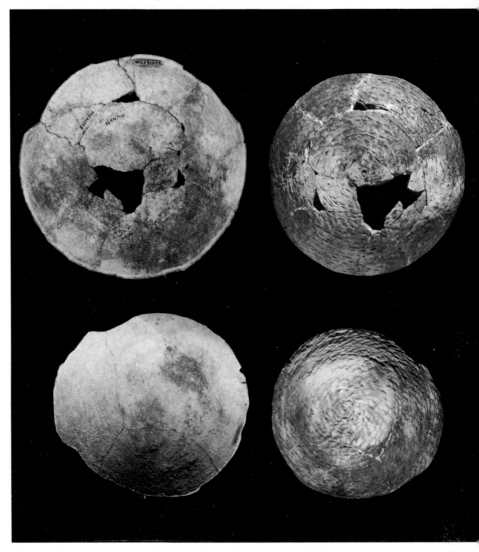

TABLE 9.—*Distribution of stone artifacts by type, Big Juniper House.*

Columns "Troughed metates" through "Crushers" fall under the heading **MILLING OR GRINDING IMPLEMENTS**.

PROVENIENCE	Troughed metates	Plain-faced metates	Plain/troughed metates	Type 1a manos	Type 1b manos	Type 1c manos	Type 1d manos	Type 2a manos	Type 2b manos	Mortars	Type 1 unspecialized milling stones	Type 2 unspecialized milling stones	Type 3 unspecialized milling stones	Type 4 unspecialized milling stones	Handstones	Crushers	Flat tabular abraders	Flat irregular abraders	Abrader from a mano fragment	Saws	Whetstone	Narrow-grooved abraders	Medium-grooved abraders	Broad-grooved abraders	Combination-grooved abraders	Rubbing stone	Polishing stone
South Trash Mound	1			12	10	4					1	1					8	1		1		2			1	1	2
East Trash Mound												1					1										
East House Mound				1							1						1						1				
Test Trench 2											1																
Test Trench 4																											
Test Trench 5																											
Test Trench 13				1		1																					
Test Trench 15	1			1	1	1									1												
Area A				1													1										
Area D	1																										
Area 11																											
Area 12	1			4	1										1		1						1				
Cist 2				3	1																						
South Trash and Cist 3					1																						
Cist 3		1		1																							
Rooms 1a and 1b, cross-wall	1																										
Rooms 1a and 1b, Level 1	1																										
Room 1a, upper fill				1	2	1										1											
Room 1b, upper fill					1																						
Room 1b, lower fill				3												1											
Room 2, fill				1	1	1					1											1		2			
Room 2, floor				2																							
Room 2, subfloor				1																							
Room 3, fill				2													1										
Room 3, subfloor					1		1																				
Area 6 (Rooms 4, 5, 24, Level 1)					1																						
Room 4, fill																											
Room 5, fill																1											
Room 5, Cist 1				6	1											1											
Room 6, fill				2	1																						
Room 6, floor																											
Room 6, subfloor																											
Room 7, fill						1										1						2	1				
Room 7, subfloor				2							1																
Room 7, subfloor cist	2																										
Room 8, fill				1																							
Room 8, floor						1																					
Room 8, subfloor	1				2								1														
Room 9, fill					2												2										
Room 9, west wall										1																	
Room 10, upper fill	1			1	1			1																			

110

Table of artifact counts — spanning headers: **FABRICATING IMPLEMENTS** | **ORNAM. AND PAINT STONES** | **ARTIFACTS OF UNCERTAIN USE**

Notched and grooved hammers	Type 1 rough hammerstones	Type 2 rough hammerstones	Type 3 rough hammerstones	Discoidal hammerstone	Pitted hammerstones	Axes	Bitted stones	Notched and grooved stones	Large core chopper	Small core choppers	Flake choppers	Other tools re-used as choppers	Scrapers	Planes	Knives or projectile points	Drills	Utilized flakes: cutting	Utilized flakes: cutting, scraping	Utilized flakes: scraping	Utilized flakes: cutting, chopping	Utilized flakes: chopping	Utilized flakes: cutting, pounding	Utilized flakes: cutting, sawing	Utilized flakes: drilling, cutting	Utilized cores	Anvils	Pendants and pendant blanks	Beads	Paint stones	Tiponi	Tabular slabs	Manolike slabs	Roughly rounded slabs	Jar lids	Tether weight	Concretions	Fossil	Other indeterminate objects	Total
		50	7	1	1		3	8		6	2	1	13	8			64	25	2	1	2			2	5				1		4			1		18	1	1	272
																	1					1																	4
1	7																4										1												17
																	1																						2
																	1																						1
	1																																						1
																																	1						3
		7	1		1		1	1		1			2	1			8	3			1			1			1		1								1		36
		2																													1								5
													2																										3
																	1																						1
		11		1									1				6				1				4						2					6			41
																															1								5
																	1																						1
1																																							3
															1																								1
											1						1																						2
	1																																						11
																	1																						2
2	1	2	1																			1																	11
		4	1									1					1																						15
		6		1													1																						11
		2	1							1							1									1													7
																																							3
																																							2
		1											1							2											1								6
	1																1																						2
																	3														1								5
					1																										2								12
1	1	3									1		1		1		3														2								14
																	1		1																				2
	1																																						1
1	1												3				4							1			1				3					1			21
		1	1																																				5
		1																																					3
															1		2														2							1	7
																																							1
		1															2										1											1	9
		2															2	1																					9
																																							1
1		1															5	1													1								13

111

The borders along the grinding surface are usually well defined but some of them, reflecting either intensive use or lack of care taken in the manufacture of the metates, are very poorly defined (fig. 97e). The parts next to the grinding surface are polished, probably as the result of constant wear by the ends of the manos.

Most of the metates are made from relatively thick sandstone slabs. Two specimens, much thicker than usual, are made from blocks or boulders of sandstone (fig. 97d and e). Another is much thinner than normal (fig. 97b) and may be related to Morris' "thin-slab" type of closed-end troughed metate with a suggested ceremonial function (Morris, 1939, p. 133, pl. 149).

No troughed metates open at both ends were found in grinding position. Room 11, which seems to have been a workroom designed for corn grinding, had several slab bins without metates; however, each bin had metate supports in place.

Troughed metates with both ends open occur primarily in late Pueblo II and probably early Pueblo III. Evidence from the sites excavated by the Wetherill Mesa Project indicates that this type of metate replaced the closed-end troughed metate at least by A.D. 1000 and probably somewhat earlier.

Plain-faced metates. Three whole plain-faced metates and two fragments were found during the excavation (fig. 97f–h). They are blocky and not as well shaped as most plain-faced metates found in later sites. Two whole metates and one fragment were made of the fine- to medium-grained sandstone. The other two specimens were made of volcanic breccia found in several dikes at Mesa Verde (fig. 97f). This material is coarse-grained and self-sharpening.

These metates are generally oval in outline. They were shaped by edge spalling or overall bifacial spalling. The grinding surface is concave excpt in one fragment, which is concave in transverse section and nearly flat in longitudinal section. Only one specimen (fig. 97g) was ground on the back. The three complete metates range in size as follows: length 32 to 41 cm.; width 23 to 24 cm.; thickness 6 to 12 cm.; and weight 7.5 to 15.8 kg.

No plain-faced metates were found in grinding position. One metate (fig. 97h) lay on the south banquette of Kiva C, and another (fig. 97f) may have been used as a deflector in Kiva A.

Plain-faced metates were probably first made in late Pueblo II or early Pueblo III, and by middle Pueblo III (around A.D. 1200) they largely replaced the troughed metates open at both ends.

Plain/troughed metates. There are three complete and three fragmentary metates of this type, all made of sandstone. Apparently, they are troughed metates, with both ends open, remodeled in the plain-faced pattern. The three complete metates show possible steps in this process. One has a well-defined border on one side of the grinding surface, with the other border spalled off (fig. 97i). Another has a ·poorly defined and partially ground-down

border on one side, while the other border has been spalled and ground off (fig. 97j). The third metate has only a slightly raised edge along each side of the grinding surface (fig. 97k).

Two of these metates are similar in shape and size to open-ended troughed metates. The other complete metate (fig. 97k) is thin and bifacially spalled and pecked around the perimeter to a rectangular outline. It may be another example of Morris' thin-slab type.

One fragment was on edge in the floor of a mealing bin (Bin 2) in Room 11 and probably served as a metate support. The other fragments and the whole specimens were found in Kiva A. The restricted distribution of this type may indicate a ceremonial function.

Manos

A mano has been defined by Woodbury (1954, p. 66) as "The tabular piece of stone held in the hands and rubbed back and forth on a metate for grinding. . . . stones used with a rotary motion are excluded."

The manos from Big Juniper House are of two types: those used on troughed metates, and a new type used both on troughed and plain-faced or plain/troughed metates. With one possible exception (fig. 98a), there were no manos used exclusively on plain-faced metates.

These tools generally show more care in manufacture than do the metates. Shaping was done by spalling and pecking and a few were ground on the sides and ends and sometimes on the backs.

Some of the manos from Big Juniper House could have been manipulated best with two hands and many more could have been used more efficiently with one hand, but I found no consistent length groupings, coupled with other observable features, to justify setting up "two-handed" and "one-handed" varieties. (The "hand-stones," described later, were undoubtedly used with one hand only.)

Type 1—Unifacial or bifacial, with grinding surface convex from end to end. Ends are usually beveled or canted from the grinding surface as a result of wear on the borders of troughed metates, which show complementary wear. Four subtypes are recognized.

Subtype 1A manos are unifacial, with the single grinding surface convex from end to end and flat to slightly convex from side to side (fig. 98).

Forty-three whole and 36 fragmentary manos were classified as Subtype 1A. Eight whole manos had finger-grips, or small depressions pecked on each side and approximately opposite each other, and four fragments had one or two finger-grips extant (fig. 98a-c). There were never more than two finger-grips, and they were always paired. Finger-grips were more likely to occur on the thicker manos.

All but five manos of this subtype were made of fine-grained sandstone, including five river cobbles. The other five manos were made from granular igneous rock (2), conglomerate (1), coarse-grained sandstone (1), and quartzite (1), and all of these are considered to be self-sharpening.

97 *Metate types: troughed metates, a–e; plain-faced, f–h; and plain/troughed, i–k. Length of a is 43.2 cm.*

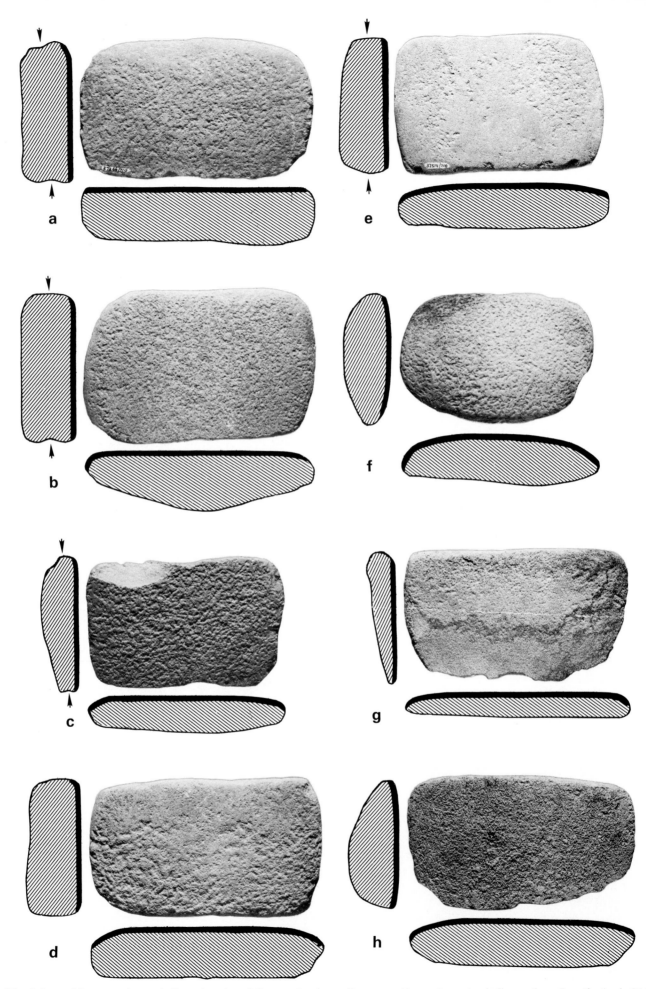

98   *Subtype 1A manos. Arrows indicate location of finger-grips, heavy lines on sections represent grinding surface. Length of a is 21.5 cm.*

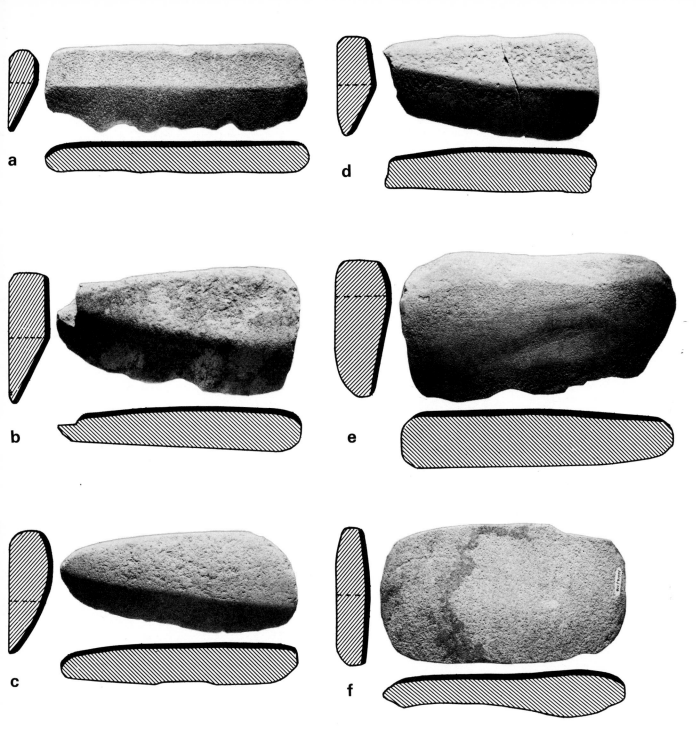

a

d

b

e

c

f

99 *Subtype 1B manos. Dashed line indicated juncture of two grinding surfaces. Length of a is 24.2 cm.*

Subtype 1A manos are subrectangular, suboval, or sub-triangular in outline. Cross sections are generally tabular or rectangular, and a few are wedge-shaped and "humpback." The humpbacks are usually not loaf-shaped—the shape typical of many late Pueblo III manos used on plain-faced metates. Almost all the manos of fine-grained sandstone were sharpened by pecking in order to make them effective grinding tools.

The following are dimensions and weights of Subtype 1A manos:

	Length (cm.)	Width (cm.)	Thickness (cm.)	Weight (kg.)
Maximum	23.8	13.9	5.9	2.6
Minimum	17.6	8.5	1.6	.6
Average	20.8	11.7	3.2	1.3

Subtype 1B manos are unifacial, with two adjacent grinding surfaces convex from end to end and more or less flat from side to side (fig. 99). The line between the grinding surfaces is either parallel or oblique to the long axis of the mano; it is sometimes very poorly defined (fig. 99f).

There were 12 whole and 25 fragmentary specimens. One complete mano has a single finger-grip and another has a finger-grip on each side. One fragment has a finger-grip on one side.

One mano fragment of volcanic breccia was self-sharpening. The rest of the fragmentary and whole manos were made of the same kind of sandstone used for the majority of Subtype 1A manos. Almost all

117

Subtype 1B manos were sharpened by pecking. One of the grinding surfaces was often worn more than the other.

Subtype 1B manos range in outline from subrectangular to suboval to subtriangular. Cross sections are usually rectangular to oblong in longitudinal section and triangular or rounded in transverse section. Subtype 1B manos are generally much thinner than those of Subtype 1A.

The following are dimensions and weights of Subtype 1B manos:

	Length (cm.)	Width (cm.)	Thickness (cm.)	Weight (kg.)
Maximum	24.7	12.9	4.5	1.7
Minimum	15.7	7.5	1.4	.4
Average	20.4	10.3	2.6	.8

Subtype 1C manos are bifacial, with the single grinding surface on each face convex from end to end and more or less flat from side to side (fig. 100). They are rectangular or, less commonly, suboval in outline. Longitudinal sections are primarily subrectangular and slightly biconvex, while the transverse sections are subrectangular or wedge-shaped.

Of the 11 whole and 17 fragmentary manos of Subtype 1C, 9 whole specimens and 14 fragments were fine-grained sandstone. One whole mano and one fragment were made of quartzite, and one whole mano was made from a coarse-grained igneous rock (fig. 100c). Two fragments were made of volcanic breccia and self-sharpening sandstone.

Four whole manos and one fragment had finger-grips. One of the four complete specimens had three finger-grips, two on one side and one on the opposite side (fig. 100a). The fragment had a single finger-grip on the thicker side. Most Subtype 1C manos had been sharpened by pecking.

The following are dimensions and weights of Subtype 1C manos:

	Length (cm.)	Width (cm.)	Thickness (cm.)	Weight (kg.)
Maximum	23.5	13.5	5.0	2.7
Minimum	11.4	8.9	2.4	.9
Average	20.1	11.4	3.5	1.2

100   *Subtype 1C manos. Arrows indicate location of finger-grips, heavy lines on sections represent grinding surfaces. Lengths: a, 11.4 cm.; b, 20.5 cm.; c, 22.3 cm.; and d, 20.1 cm.*

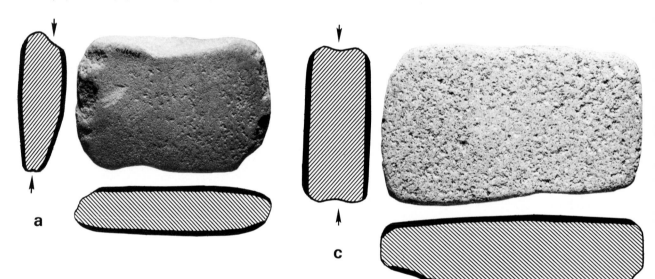

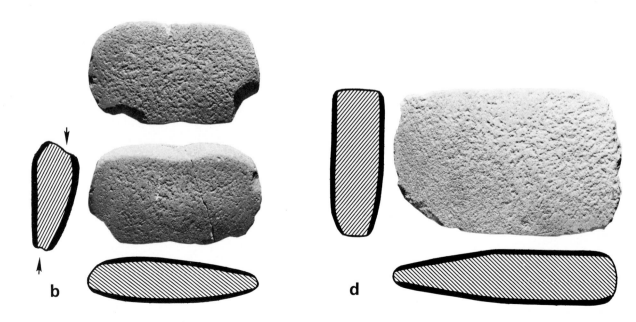

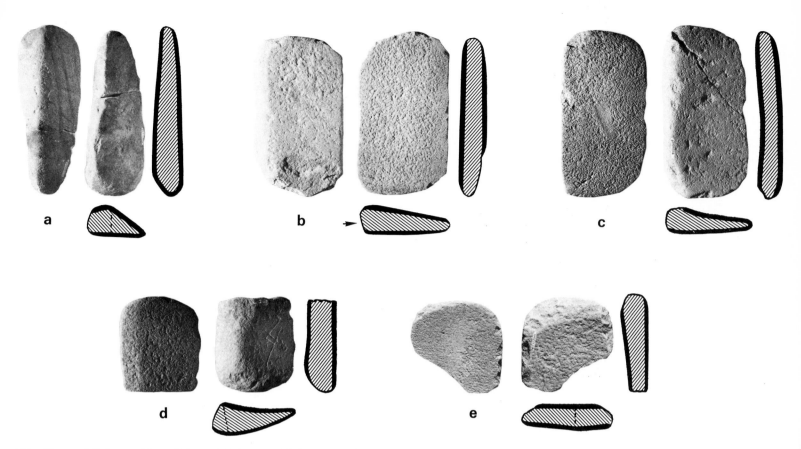

101 *Manos of Subtype 1D, a; Subtype 2A, b, c; and Subtype 2B, d, e. Arrow indicates location of finger-grip, heavy lines show grinding surfaces. Length of a is 21.8 cm.*

Subtype 1D is represented by one bifacial mano with two grinding surfaces on one face and one grinding surface on the opposite face (fig. 101a). It is convex in longitudinal section and flat to slightly convex in transverse section. The ends are markedly and slightly beveled or canted from the face with the single grinding surface but not from the other face.

Made of fine-grained sandstone, this mano is subtriangular in outline. Two of the grinding surfaces are worn fairly smooth and the third has been sharpened by pecking. A pecked area on part of the thicker side may have served as a finger-grip. Measurements are: length 21.8 cm., width 8.5 cm., maximum thickness 3.5 cm., and weight 0.6 kg.

Type 2—Bifacial, with grinding surfaces which are convex or concave from end to end. Two subtypes are recognized.

Subtype 2A manos have two grinding surfaces, each; one of these is convex from end to end, and the other is concave from end to end (fig. 101b and c). The four manos of this subtype may have started as unifacial manos used on troughed metates, and were later turned over and used on plain-faced or plain/troughed metates. There is reason to believe that the three metate types were used simultaneously during the latter part of the occupation of Big Juniper House. It follows that all the mano types were used simultaneously during this time.

Three of the manos were made of the sandstone apparently preferred in the majority of manos and metates. The fourth was made of the self-sharpening variety of sandstone (fig. 101c). One mano had a single finger-grip

(fig. 101b) on the thicker side, and may have had one on the other side before it was worn thin.

One grinding surface is convex longitudinally and flat to convex transversely; ends are beveled or canted from use on troughed metates. The opposite grinding surface is concave longitudinally and flat to slightly concave to slightly convex, from use on plain-faced or plain/troughed metates; ends are not beveled or canted. All grinding surfaces show sharpening by pecking. The ranges of dimensions and weights of Subtype 2A manos are: length 16.3–22.2 cm.; width 8.8–12.0 cm.; thickness 2.4–3.3 cm.; and weight 0.6–1.1 kg.

Subtype 2B manos, represented by two fragments, had three grinding surfaces, two on one face and one on the opposite face (fig. 101d and e). The two grinding surfaces on one face are convex from end to end and flat to slightly convex from side to side, from use on troughed metates. The single grinding surface on the opposite face is concave longitudinally and slightly concave transversely, from use on a plain-faced or plain/troughed metates.

Both specimens are made of the common fine-grained sandstone. They had been sharpened by pecking, and they lacked finger-grips. Measurements are: 12.8 and 12.0 cm. wide and 2.4 and 3.5 cm. thick, respectively.

Two manos of this subtype were found at Badger House and a number of Type 2 manos were excavated by the Awatovi Expedition at Antelope Mesa sites in northeastern Arizona (Woodbury, 1954, p. 68). Some of these manos have one flat grinding surface opposite the convex one, but they were found in contexts earlier than flat metates (classified as plain-faced metates here). Woodbury suggests that these manos were used on grinding slabs, or that they were ground on one face, either to provide an area to be used as a whetstone or to improve their appearance. However, he believes that manos with two flat grinding surfaces opposite the convex one were used first on troughed metates and then on flat metates.

Mortars

Two stone artifacts, with one circular, pecked and ground depression, each, were classified as mortars. One of these (fig. 102, left), a possible sandstone concretion, measures 10.1 by 9.8 by 3.1 cm., and weighs 5 kg. The depression is 6.5 cm. in diameter and 0.9 cm. deep. The other mortar (fig. 102, right) is a sandstone block measuring 21 by 16.8 by 8.7 cm., and weighing 4.2 kg. The depression is 7.5 cm. in diameter and 1.1 cm. in depth.

Unspecialized Milling Stones

Twenty-two grinding tools from Big Juniper House that were obviously used as netherstones are designated as "unspecialized milling stones." Their function was not necessarily restricted to food preparation, as metates are thought to have been, and, unlike metates and mortars, their shapes are purely fortuitous. Suggested functions for these artifacts, aside from possible use in grinding food, are preparation of pigment and grinding rocks or sherds for pottery temper. Four types are recognized on the basis of their grinding surfaces.

Type 1—Unifacial or bifacial, with concave grinding surface. Of the 14 specimens of this type, 11 complete

102 *Mortars. Mortar at left is 10.1 cm. in maximum diameter; one at right is 21 cm. in length.*

103 *Unspecialized milling stones, Type 1. Side fragment of a metate, e; possible basin metate, g; bifacial unspecialized mill stone with paint stain on visible face, h. Length of a is 22.5 cm.*

and 2 fragmentary examples are unifacial and one complete specimen is bifacial (fig. 103h). Twelve are made of the common sandstone; half of these were sharpened by pecking, and the others were worn smooth. The remaining two specimens were made of self-sharpening, coarse-grained igneous rock (fig. 103d) and volcanic breccia.

These milling stones are subrectangular or suboval in outline. They could be held in the lap or, in the case of several of the smaller ones, in one hand of the person doing the grinding.

The single bifacial milling stone has a red paint stain on one grinding surface, and a fragmentary specimen, the modified side fragment of a plain/troughed metate, also has a paint stain on the grinding surface (fig. 103e).

One Type 1 specimen has a deep concave grinding surface and may have been a "basin metate"—a type of milling stone that is rarely found in the Mesa Verde area (fig. 103g).

One complete troughed metate and two troughed metate fragments had small concave grinding surfaces on the face opposite the grinding surface.

The following are dimensions and weights of Type 1 unspecialized milling stones:

	Length (cm.)	Width (cm.)	Thickness (cm.)	Weight (kg.)
Maximum	28.3	20.4	9.0	20.2
Minimum	14.2	11.0	2.2	.7
Average	22.1	14.1	4.9	6.3

Type 2—Re-used manos, with concave grinding surface. The two specimens, both complete, were originally Subtype 1A manos (fig. 104a and b). Both were made of the common sandstone and were sharpened by pecking. They could have been held in the lap or in one hand during use.

Type 3—Unifacial, with flat grinding surface. The three complete examples were made of the common sandstone (fig. 104c–e). Two are subrectangular and one is semicircular in outline. They were worn smooth or fairly smooth with use. One of the rectangular specimens was carefully ground on the sides, ends, and back (fig. 104c). The other rectangular milling stone had a red paint stain on the grinding surface (fig. 104e).

Type 4—Bifacial, with flat and concave grinding surfaces. The three specimens, subrectangular in outline, were made of the common sandstone (fig. 104f–h). One is ground on all edges and faces (fig. 104h), and another is bifacially spalled and ground on the perimeter (fig. 104f).

104 *Unspecialized milling stones. Type 2, a, b; Type 3, c–e; Type 4, f–h. Length of a is 18.7 cm; length of g, not to scale, is 21.5 cm.*

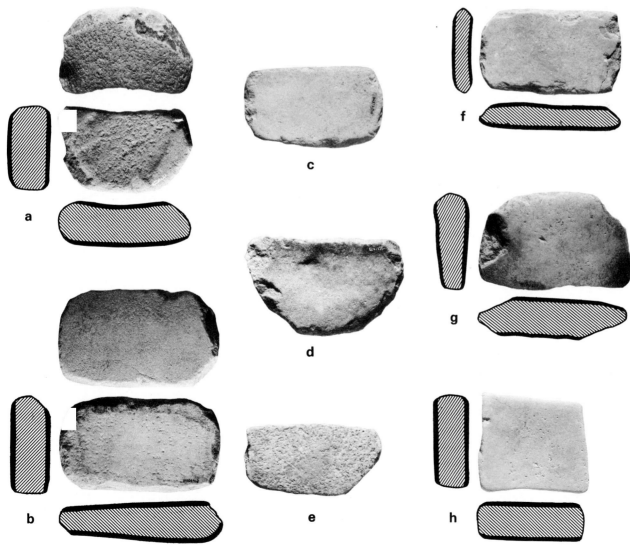

Handstones

Eight oval grinding implements were classified as handstones (fig. 105). It is assumed that they were used primarily with unspecialized milling stones. However, the discovery of a handstone in association with a troughed metate at Two Raven House on Wetherill Mesa suggests that handstones were used, at least part of the time, with metates.

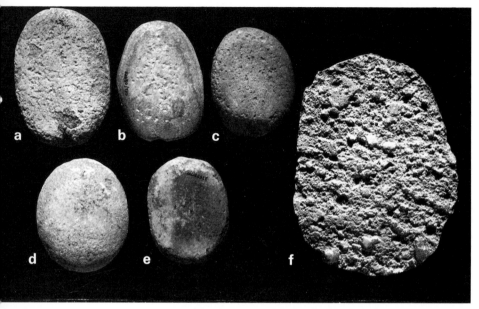

105 *Handstones. Cobble handstones, a–e. Length of a is 12.8 cm. Braccia handstone, f, is 13.9 cm. in length.*

106 *Crushers. Length of a is 23 cm.*

Seven of the handstones are complete and one is fragmentary. Six of them are quartzitic sandstone; one is of a sandstone which is much harder than that of most metates and manos; and one is a very coarse-grained igneous breccia (fig. 105f). The sandstone specimens are stream cobbles showing little modification. The breccia handstone is from quarried material and has been shaped by spalling.

Since grinding striations on the handstones are usually not alined in one direction, it seems likely that most of these tools were used with a rotary motion. None of the handstones show much wear and most of them show secondary use as hammerstones, with the perimeter lightly battered and pecked. One specimen has a possible fingergrip in the middle of each side (fig. 105e). Two handstones are unifacial, the other six are bifacial. There is only one grinding surface on a face. Their sizes suggest they were used with one hand.

The following are dimensions and weights of handstones:

	Length (cm.)	Width (cm.)	Thickness (cm.)	Weight (kg.)
Maximum	13.9	10.3	6.2	0.85
Minimum	10.2	7.7	2.2	.54
Average	11.5	8.8	4.1	.63

Crushers

Nine subrectangular grinding tools—eight complete and one fragmentary—are distinguishable from manos and handstones by their greater massiveness (fig. 106). They have been tentatively designated as "crushers" on the assumption that they were used to pulverize hard materials for tempering.

a

b

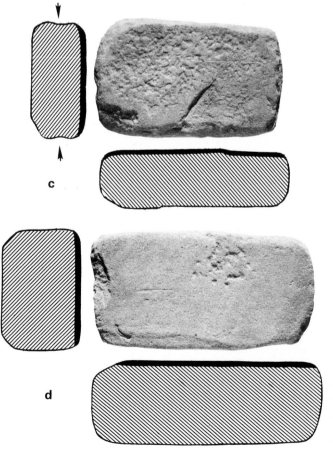

c

d

Seven specimens are of hard-grained sandstone, one of quartzite, and one of sedimentary conglomerate (fig. 106a). They were shaped by spalling and pecking. One is bifacial and the rest are unifacial. The grinding surfaces vary from slightly convex to flat, and most of them show evidence of sharpening by pecking. One complete crusher (fig. 106c) has one finger-grip on each side. The bifacial crusher has a finger-grip on one side. None of them show the characteristic wear facet at the ends of the grinding surface typical of manos used on troughed metates.

The following are dimensions and weights of crushers:

	Length (cm.)	Width (cm.)	Thickness (cm.)	Weight (kg.)
Maximum	25.6	14.2	7.6	4.5
Minimum	18.5	11.2	4.7	2.4
Average	22.7	12.9	6.4	3.3

FABRICATING IMPLEMENTS

Stone artifacts were presumably used in the manufacture or preparation of other tools, or in the shaping of building stones. These have been categorized as fabricating implements.

107 *Abrading stones. Tabular flat abraders, a–e, h–j; irregular flat abraders, f, g; and abrader from mano fragment, k. Length of a is 12.2 cm.*

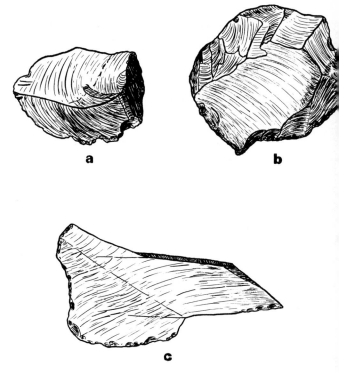

130 *Utilized flakes: sawing, a; cutting and drilling, b; and cutting and punching, c. Length of c is 6.1 cm.*

Utilized Cores

Fourteen cores were utilized for cutting, chopping, and scraping, or combinations of these functions (fig. 131). Materials used were chert or claystone (13), and quartzite (1). Sections are planoconvex (7), biconvex (3), triangular (1), irregular (1), wedge-shaped (1), and flat (1). Outlines are suboval (4), subtriangular (3), irregular (2), discoidal (2), and pyramidal, ovate, and five-sided (1 each).

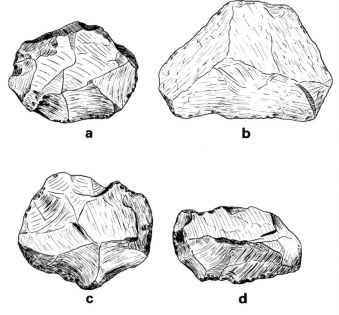

131 *Utilized cores. Length of b is 8.4 cm.*

129 *Utilized flakes: chopping, a, b; cutting and chopping, c; and cutting, scraping, and pounding, d. Length of a is 6 cm.*

had been chipped by use in cutting and scraping, and blunted through use in pounding (fig. 129d).

Sawing flake. One chert flake with a serrated edge indicated a sawing function (fig. 130a). The "teeth" were slightly worn, as would be expected if the flake had been used for sawing. It is suboval in outline and planoconvex in longitudinal and transverse sections. Measurements are 3.7 by 2.5 by 1.1 cm., and weight is 67 gm.

Drilling and cutting flakes. Two chert flakes had worn and dulled points in addition to chipped edges, indicating use for drilling as well as cutting. The upper margins next to the points were also worn and slightly polished as if used for drills. A quadrilateral-shaped flake had an irregular cross section and measured 3.8 by 2.1 by 1.0 cm., and weighed 6 gm. A discoidal-shaped flake (fig. 130b) had planoconvex sections; it measured 4.6 by 3.7 by 1.2 cm., and weighed 21 gm.

Cutting and punching flake. One chert flake, irregular-shaped with flat sections, had a sharp point which was probably used for punching in addition to having edges for cutting purposes (fig. 130c). It measures 6.1 by 2.9 by 0.6 cm., and weighs 13 gm.

The following are measurements and weights of utilized cores:

	Length (cm.)	Width (cm.)	Thickness (cm.)	Weight (gm.)
Maximum	8.4	5.9	3.5	127
Minimum	3.1	3.1	1.7	23
Average	5.4	4.2	2.7	67

132 *Anvils. Length of lower artifact is 20.5 cm.*

Anvils

Three irregular-shaped cobbles of quartzitic sandstone were classified as anvils (fig. 132). The faces were pecked and battered (one had scratches in a restricted area), as if they had been used as platforms. Measurements are: lengths 11.7, 13.4, and 20.5 cm.; widths 10.2, 11.2, and 8.8 cm.; thickness 6.1, 5.2, and 5.5 cm.; and weights 1.0, 1.2, and 1.5 kg.

ORNAMENTS AND PAINT STONES

Ornaments

Rectangular pendants, perforated at one end. Three pendants, with a perforation drilled through one end (fig. 133a–c), and one pendant, with a hole started in one end (fig. 133d), are rectangular. The first three were ground on both faces and all edges. The perforations were biconically drilled, with the apices meeting in the center. All are made of orange to red shale.

Subcircular pendant. One pendant of buff travertine, subcircular in outline, has a perforation at the center (fig. 133g). Both faces and the perimeter were ground smooth. The perforation was biconically drilled.

Pendant blanks. Two ground, red shale specimens of approximately rectangular shape are probably pendant blanks (fig. 133e and f). One (fig. 133e) was ground on both faces and all edges. The other was ground on one face and one side only. Neither was perforated.

Beads. Three beads of three different styles were found. One is an annular bead of brown stone, 0.6 cm. in diameter and 0.4 cm. thick. It is polished and ground on both faces and around the perimeter. The biconically drilled hole is 0.2 cm. in diameter.

Another is made of azurite, oval in outline, with a narrow, V-shaped groove around the middle. It is ground over the entire surface. The dimensions are 0.6 by 0.4 by 0.4 cm.

The third bead, also of azurite, is spheroidal, with dimensions of 0.7 by 0.6 by 0.4 cm. It is ground over the entire surface. This may have been an inlay piece, as there is no groove or perforation for stringing. The two azurite beads were found together in the floor fill of Kiva A (table 9).

Paint Stones

Eight mineral stones are classified as paint stones (fig. 134). One or more surfaces have been chipped or ground to obtain pigment, probably for use in decorating pottery or other artifacts, or for wall painting or body decoration. Several unspecialized milling stones and pottery sherds described previously have traces of pigment, probably from the grinding of paint stones and mixing the pigment.

The paint stones are: hematite (6), two purple, three red, one red-brown; limonite (1), yellow-orange; limonite and hematite (1), yellow-red. Shapes are oblong (1), subtriangular (4), and variable (1). Measurements are: length 3.1 to 4.2 cm.; width 2.5 to 4.0 cm.; thickness 1.4 to 2.6 cm.; and weight 36 to 122 gm.

CEREMONIAL OBJECT

Only one stone artifact was identified, with any degree of certainty, as a ceremonial object (fig. 135). It is a conical sandstone block. Similar objects have been called *tiponis,* corn goddess symbols, corn ears, earth mothers, and, by Judd (1954, p. 295), "Mountain Lion, hunter of the north."

The specimen from Big Juniper House has an oval, relatively flat base that was ground and pecked. The rest of the surface was ground smooth except for part of the surface near the apex, which had been spalled off. It measures 24.0 cm. long by 23.0 cm. maximum width by 17.2 cm. thick, and weighs approximately 10.3 kg. It was found on its side on the floor of the floor-level ventilator tunnel of Kiva A, and was apparently placed there intentionally.

Roberts (1932, p. 143, pl. 55 d and e) illustrates several conical stone objects that were found in the Village of the Great Kivas in New Mexico. These appear to be quite similar to the one found at Big Juniper House and to others found on Wetherill Mesa and elsewhere in Mesa Verde National Park (Fewkes, 1911, p. 67). Morris (1939, pp. 129–130, pl. 137) reports finding "Corn Goddess" symbols from Sites 39 and 41 on the La Plata River

133 *Pendants and pendant blanks. Length of a is 6.4 cm.*

which are the same type of artifact as the one from Big Juniper House. Parsons (1939) makes several references to the use of *tiponis* in the ceremonial life of the present-day Pueblos. Although the construction of these speci- mens is not described, most of them are of clay or wood, sometimes of hide, with perforations for attaching prayer sticks or feathers. They have the conical shape of the prehistoric stone objects.

Slabs

Slabs were classified according to shape. The four types recognized are tabular, manolike, and roughly rounded slabs, and jar lids.

Tabular slabs. Thirty-two slabs are tabular and usually subrectangular in shape. Other shapes are trapezoidal (1), five-sided (1), and quadrilateral (1). Sixteen were interminate because of their fragmentary nature. All were of sandstone. Usually one face was ground, sometimes both, but rarely would neither face be ground. Sides were usually bifacially chipped, some were ground over the chipping.

Slabs of this type were probably used as door slabs, cist covers, cooking slabs, ventilator-tunnel doors in kivas, mealing-bin walls, and for other purposes. A probable door slab and a smaller slab that covered a cist in Kiva C are shown in figure 136a and b. Measurements are: length 12.0 to 60.4 cm.; width 8.1 to 42.0 cm.; thickness 0.6 to 3.0 cm.; and weight 0.7 to 10.9 kg.

Manolike slabs. Four sandstone slabs are manolike in thickness and shape but do not have the grinding surfaces or beveled ends of manos (fig. 136c). One or both faces are ground on the high spots, giving an uneven appearance to the faces. Only one slab is complete. Measurements are: length 12.0 to 24.0 cm.; width 12.2 to 13.4 cm.; and thickness 3.4 to 5.1 cm. The complete specimen weighs 2.3 kg.

Roughly rounded slabs. Three fragmentary slabs were roughly rounded. They would seem to be too large to serve as jar lids and are not as well made (see below). Two of the specimens have one face ground and one face unmodified. The third slab has both faces unmodified. One fragment has the edge bifacially chipped and the other two have edges ground over spalling. All are made of sandstone. The most complete of the three specimens (fig. 136d) measures 26.1+ cm. long by 20.7 cm. wide by 2.8 cm. thick.

Jar lids. Three complete slabs and one fragment have been classified as jar lids because of their fine workmanship and generally discoidal shape (fig. 136e–g). One specimen is hexagonal. Usually both faces are ground flat and the edges are bifacially chipped with some grinding. Three of them are sandstone and one is mottled gray-black shale. Although I have termed them jar lids, actually none was found covering a jar, but similar slabs from other sites have been found in such associations. One of the jar lids (fig. 136g) may have covered the sipapu in Kiva C.

One irregular slab, unworked in any way except for the initial spalling, was found covering a jar set in the floor of Room 6.

Tether Weight

A soft, gritty, maul-shaped sandstone object has a pecked groove around the middle (fig. 137). It was roughly shaped by spalling on most of the surface; it

134 *Paint stones. Length of d is 3.9 cm.*

135 *Ceremonial object.*

139 *Concretion balls. Length of a is 8.1 cm.*

140 *Concretions—possible pot supports. Length of concretion at left is 13.9 cm.*

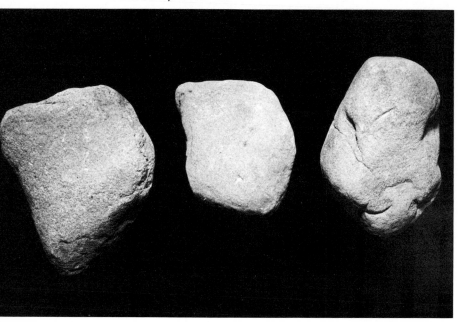

tishes. Thirty-three concretions had the following shapes: cylinders or constricted cones (10), balls (8), lobate forms (5), disks (3), flat "bars" (3), dish-shaped (1), and irregular (3) (figs. 138 and 139).

Of the nine concretions found in the kivas, three were mudded in the walls of the Kiva C firepit (fig. 140, right), one was next to the firepit in the Kiva B floor (fig. 141, left), one was on the Kiva A floor (fig. 141, right), and the rest were in fill close to the floors of Kivas A and B. Two are "bird" or "foot and ankle" shapes; the others are more or less irregular.

The term "pot supports" has been suggested to describe stones similar to these nine concretions, but there is little or no evidence to suggest such a function. All have been burned to varying degrees and therefore may have been used in firepits. However, they were found only in kivas and there were firepits in other areas of the site. They may have served as firedogs, supports for wood in the hearths. Two of these objects supported a large slab in a kiva in Mug House.

Fossil

The fragment of a fossil mollusk, found in the South Trash Mound, appears to be unmodified.

Other Indeterminate Objects

The five objects of indeterminate use are illustrated and described individually.

Figure 142a. End fragment. Brownish-gray, coarse-grained igneous rock, probably from one of the exposed dikes in the park. One face ground flat, opposite face unmodified. Sides pecked, with possible finger-grip on one side. Width 16.4 cm. and thickness 6.6 cm. May be a broken handstone.

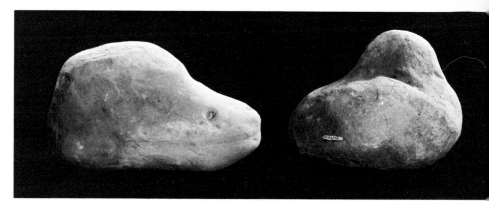

141 *Concretions—bird shaped "pot supports." Length of concretion at left is 16.9 cm.*

a

b

c

d   e

142 *Indeterminate objects.*

Figure 142b. Complete. Buff sandstone. Subtriangular in outline and subrectangular in sections. One face ground and pecked, opposite face spalled with some pecking on high spots. Narrower end and one side pecked, other end and side bifacially chipped and pecked. Measurements: 28.8 by 13.6 by 3.8 cm., and weight 2.1 kg.

Figure 142c. Complete. Reddish-brown sandstone. Suboval in outline. One face convex, ground and pecked (sharpened?); opposite face uneven, pecked on high spots. Sides pecked, ends are spalled and partly pecked. Measurements: 20.8 by 13.4 by 4.0 cm., and weight 1.9 kg. Possibly a mano, but it is definitely atypical in shape

and workmanship.

Figure 142d. Complete(?). Petrified wood, yellow-buff in color. Subrectangular in outline and sections. Faces, sides, and one end have been ground fairly smooth and flat; other end possibly broken. Measurements: 5.0 by 3.3 by 1.2 cm., and weight 25 gm.

Figure 142e. Complete. Black, fine-grained chert or claystone. Subrectangular in outline and transverse section, and wedge-shaped in longitudinal section. Faces and one end ground and polished. "Bit" at other end partly flaked and partly ground and polished. Measurements: 6.1 by 3.1 by 1.3 cm., and weight 53 gm.

Femur scraper. A scraper made from the left femur of an immature mule deer was found in Kiva B, as part of the probable tool kit mentioned previously (fig. 149i). The cancellous bone of the femoral crest was ground smooth and the surfaces of the shaft were polished. The curved working end was worn and use-polished, and the diagonal cut on the anterior was ground and use-polished (fig. 155a, lower). Striations on the long axis indicate the use was forward and backward. The scraper is 19.0 cm. long and 3.3 cm. in diameter below the joint.

This is the only femur scraper found by the Wetherill Mesa Project. The usual scraper of this form is made from a bighorn or mule deer humerus and retains the joint as a grip.

Humerus scraper. This scraper, made from a section of the left humerus of an adult mule deer, is represented by part of the working or leading edge showing striations on the vertical axis. The shaft was polished, and it was worn by use on the cut anterior side. No measurements of it were taken.

157 *Knife-like object, a, and problematical objects, b–d, of mammal bone. Length of a is 15.7 cm.*

a b c d

Tibia scraper. A scraper was made from the right tibia, minus the epiphysis, of a large immature mule deer (fig. 155b). The split shaft retains part of the distal articular head. Except for the original splitting and some use-polish, the joint is unmodified. The split surface of the shaft is sharply beveled toward the leading edge, and shows extensive use-polish and wear. The unsplit surface has a low bevel, and the leading edge is highly use-polished and worn. The scraper is 8.8 cm. long and 2.8 cm. wide at the joint. The leading edge is 1.1 cm. wide and 0.4 cm. thick. The shaft is 1.3 cm. thick just below the joint.

Possible scrapers. Three mule deer rib artifacts—a left central rib (fig. 156a), a left fourth or fifth rib (fig. 156b), and a right fourth rib (fig. 156c)—were classified as possible scrapers. The ribs are whole; one end is cut and the other is ground.

Two specimens (fig. 156a and c) show cancellous tissue on both edges, probably from use-grinding. One of these is ground from the ground end about two-thirds of the way along the shaft on one edge and about one-fourth of the way on the opposite edge. The other is ground on the edges about a third of the way along both edges and use-polished elsewhere. The surfaces are not modified. They may be side scrapers.

The other specimen (fig. 156b) shows a bevel from both surfaces at one end and wear on one edge (left edge in the figure). The bevel is ground into the cancellous tissue and the edge is worn just into the cancellous tissue. The opposite end has been cut diagonally and ground. There are several striations with no apparent alinement on both surfaces near the beveled end. This is a possible end scraper.

The longest artifact measures 21.0 by 1.8 cm., and is 0.4 to 0.6 cm. thick. The others measure 16.7 by 2.1 cm. and 15.0 by 1.9 cm., and are 0.5 to 0.6 cm. thick.

Knifelike object. The split shaft of the left tibia of a large adult mule deer has been classified as a knifelike object (fig. 157a). One end, cut and worn obliquely, was beveled on both surfaces. The other end was broken or cut and use-polished. The beveled end shows a high degree of wear and use-polish. The split surface and edges and the unsplit surface show some use-polish.

The object is 15.7 cm. long, 2.4 cm. wide, and 0.2 to 0.5 cm. thick. It is somewhat similar to the "skinning tool(?)" from Pecos described and illustrated by Kidder (1932, p. 242 and fig. 202i).

Probable Ornaments

Perforated mammal tibias. Three left and three right tibias of black-tailed jackrabbit (*Lepus californicus*), found in the fill of Kiva B, belong to a class of artifacts encountered at many sites in the Mesa Verde area. The artifacts are referred to, noncommittally as "perforated mammal tibias." Three of the present specimens are nearly complete (fig. 158); however, the other three are fragmentary.

Perforated mammal tibias exhibit three features. The proximal joint is ground horizontally and cored verti-

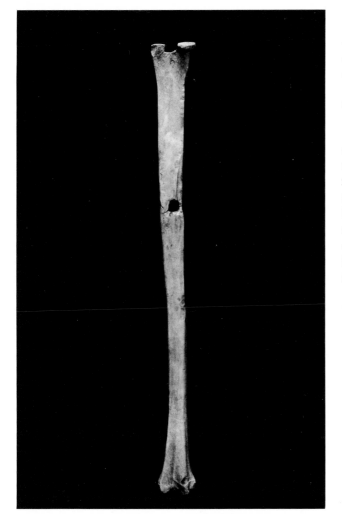

158 *Perforated mammal tibia. Length is 13.4 cm.*

The beads were made of whole shaft sections without retention of joints. The shaft surface is polished and both ends are cut and ground, and usually polished. Three beads show cut marks near one end. The rabbit bone bead is, as far as I know, unique to this area.

Tool Blank

The right metatarsal 3–4 of mule deer shows grooves cut or sawed on the dorsal and ventral surfaces, beginning near the distal foramen and running through the proximal joint. Cut marks just below the dorsal foramen of the distal joint indicate that the ligaments were served before the grooves were made (fig. 160). The specimen measures 23.7 cm. in length and 1.3 to 2.3 cm. in diameter between the joints. Presumably the shaft would have been split and tools would have been fashioned from the sections.

cally down to the marrow cavity; the shaft has a small hole drilled into the marrow cavity below the proximal end; the shaft, except for the perforation, and the distal joint are unmodified. In our group, the shaft hole is drilled in the dorsal surface in three cases, the ventral surface in two cases, and in the lateral ridge in one instance. The illustrated specimens range from 12.3 to 13.4 cm. in length and measure about 0.8 cm. in diameter between the joints.

A perforated tibia in the Mesa Verde Museum collections has a knotted piece of yucca cord passing through the shaft perforation and up through the reamed end. Possibly all such artifacts were similarly equipped with cords. There is no telling whether, as has been suggested, they functioned as ornaments or tinklers. But their frequent association with kivas implies some ceremonial purpose (table 10).

Tubular beads. Nine bone beads were found (fig. 159). Seven of them were made of turkey bones, one of a bone from an unidentified species of the order Galliformes (fig. 159c), and one from the left tibia of an unidentified species of rabbit. The bird bone specimens were made from the following elements: left ulna (3); right ulna (1); left radius (2); left tibiotarsus (1); right tibiotarsus (1). The nine beads range from 3.1 to 7.4 cm. and average about 4.9 cm. in length, and vary from 0.6 to 1.2 cm. and average 0.9 cm. in maximum diameter.

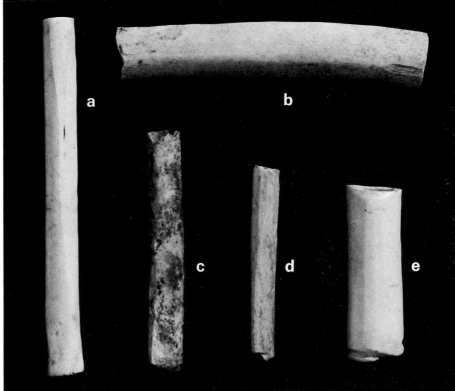

159 *Tubular beads of turkey bone. Length of a is 6.3 cm.*

160 *Tool blank of mammal bone.*

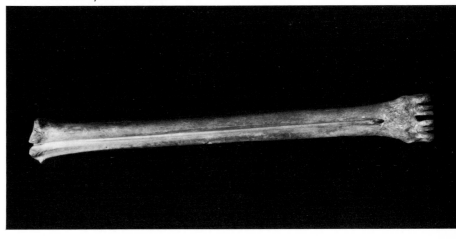

Problematical Objects

Several artifacts of bird and mammal bones cannot be placed in the preceding categories.

1. A cervical vertabra of turkey, measuring 3.6 by 2.4 by 1.4 cm., from the floor fill of Kiva A (fig. 161). Modified only by grinding at one end, this object may have been an unusual form of bead. Lyndon L. Hargrave, who has studied bird bone artifacts from many Southwestern sites, has never seen a comparable specimen.

2. The right tibiotarsus of a small adult turkey (fig. 162). It measures 16.5 cm. in length and 0.8 to 1.1 cm. in diameter between the joints. Both ends were ground, but there are no other modifications. The purpose of this object, which also came from the floor fill of Kiva A, is unknown.

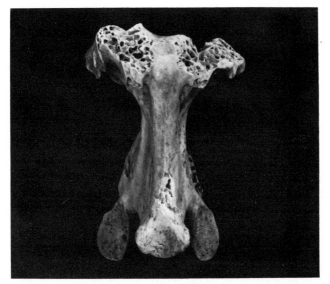

161 *Problematical object of turkey bone.*

162 *Problematical object of turkey bone.*

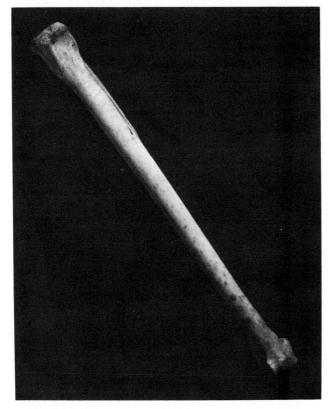

3. A longitudinally split mammal rib with one intact end (fig. 157b). The face shown is polished and the reverse, with some cancellous tissue exposed, is slightly ground. The intact end is bifacially ground to a sharp edge, and the rounded sides are ground or worn smooth. The right side, as shown in the illustration, has three shallow but well-defined grooves along the edge. The sharply constricting sides may indicate that there was a point at this end.

4. A longitudinally split mammal long bone with one partially intact end and contracting sides (fig. 157c). The face shown is ground and partly polished, and the reverse, with considerable cancellous tissue exposed, is ground fairly smooth. This object, like (3), is broken where the sides sharply constrict, presumably to form a long, tapering point.

The two artifacts just described were found in Room 5. They may be fragmentary awl spatulas (Kidder, 1932, p. 222 and fig. 187).

5. A longitudinally split mammal rib with a partly intact pointed end, found in Test Trench 1 (fig. 157d). Both the face shown and the reverse (with cancellous tissue exposed) are partly ground. The rounded sides are ground or worn smooth, and the edge of the pointed end is rounded by grinding or wear except at the very tip, which is bifacially ground and sharp. Worn grooves or notches along both sides suggest that this object may have been a weaving tool.

Fragmentary Artifacts

A number of bone artifacts in the collection were too fragmentary to be classified.

Bird bone. Three incomplete bird bone artifacts include two splinter fragments of turkey tibiotarsi and one whole shaft fragment of the left radius from an unknown species of Galliformes.

Mammal bone. Ten fragmentary artifacts of mammal bone consist of: unknown artiodactyl (3), unknown mammal (2), mule deer (4), and unknown deer (1). Three are split-shaft fragments retaining joints—a right metatarsal 3–4, with the proximal head; a metatarsal 3–4, side unknown, with the distal head; and a metacarpal 3–4, side unknown, with part of the lateral condyle. Six specimens are split-shaft sections or splinters of the following elements: right tibia (1); right metacarpal 3–4 (1); metapodial 3–4, side unknown (1); long bone fragment (2); and right rib (1). The remaining artifact is a section of the right innominate of mule deer.

TEXTILE REMAINS

The only textile remains recovered from Big Juniper House consisted of some burned fragments of matting found with Burial 6 on the floor of Room 8 (ch. 7). The matting was an over 2, under 2 twilled fabric of rush (*Scirpus* sp.), with the elements measuring 0.4 cm. in width. No selvage sections were present. Burial 6 is probably early Pueblo III, and dates about A.D. 1100.

TABLE 14.—HUMAN BONE PATHOLOGIES, BIG JUNIPER HOUSE

BURIAL	Etiologic Grouping					Abnormality	Sex	Age
	Prenatal	Growth	Degenerative	Trauma	Unclassified			
Burial 1						None	?	Adolescent.
Burial 2						None	♀	Adolescent.
Burial 3		x				50° bilateral anteversion of the femora	♀	Early teens.
Burial 4						None	♀	Adult.
Burial 5						None	♂	30–35.
Burial 6						None	?	Adult.
Burial 8	x		x	x		Scapula, perforation of the blade; arthritis of lumbar vertebrae; healed fracture of the right clavicle.	♂	30–35.
Burial 9			x	x		Arthritis; fracture dislocation of lumbar vertebrae	♂	35–40.
Burial 10						None	♀	Adolescent.
Burial 11	x		x	x		Perforation of 5th lumbar vertebral isthmus; arthritis of vertebrae; lateral compression fracture of a lumbar vertebra.	♂	35–40.
Burial 12					x	Porosis of the skull	?	Infant.
Burial 13					x	Porosis of the skull	?	Infant.
Burial 14						None	♂	Adolescent.
Burial 15						None	♀	Late teens.
Burial 16						None	?	Infant.
Burial 17		x	x			External torsion of the tibia, 30°; glenoid arthritis; arthritis of elbow; arthritis of vertebrae.	♂	30–35.
Burial 18						None	?	Infant.
Burial 19						None	♀	Adolescent.
Burial 20						None	♀?	Adult.
Burial 21						None	?	Adult.
Burial 22						None	♀?	Adult.
Burial 23			x			Acetabular arthritis	♂	Adolescent.
Burial 24			x			Acetabular arthritis	♀	Over 40.
Miscellaneous (31767/710)			x			Arthritis of the vertebrae	?	Adult.
Miscellaneous (31775/710)			x			Patellar arthritis	?	Adult.
Miscellaneous (33554/710)					x	Porosis of the skull	?	Child.

Total prenatal abnormalities=2.
Total growth abnormalities=2.
Total degenerative abnormalities=8.
Total trauma abnormalities=3.
Total unclassified abnormalities=3.

In the burial descriptions and in table 15, the following terms describing body position will be used:

Flexed burial: Burial is tightly flexed with knees drawn up to the chest and the arms usually sharply bent at the elbows, the elbows at the chest region.

Semiflexed burial: Knees at about right angles to the trunk; arms either tightly flexed or partially flexed in the same manner as the legs. Sometimes the arms are extended.

Extended burial: Legs fully extended and straight; arms usually more or less straight, but may be bent or flexed.

No clear pattern emerged as to orientation of the body, or the side upon which the head or body rested (table 15). Most of the burials were either flexed or semiflexed. One was probably extended and eight were too scattered or fragmentary to determine body position.

Sixteen of the 23 burials had associated grave goods. The number of objects ranged from one (seven burials) to nine (Burial 4). Three burials had two artifacts, two burials had three, and three burials had four, each. The usual grave offering was pottery. Burial 4 had a "killed" bowl over the skull. To my knowledge, this is the only killed-bowl burial recorded in the Mesa Verde region.

All crania that were sufficiently preserved showed asymmetrical lambdoidal deformation, probably produced by cradleboard pressure. Unfortunately, there is no information as to which side of the skull was flattened. Occipital deformation, observed on crania at several Wetherill Mesa sites, was not found at Big Juniper House.

In three burials, most of the teeth were missing and those remaining were heavily worn. Moderate to heavy tooth wear was also noted in all individuals with perma-

TABLE 15.—BURIAL PATTERNS, BIG JUNIPER HOUSE

BURIAL	Orientation					Head Position					Body Position						Grave goods associated	Sex	Age [1]
	Head to south	Head to north	Head to east	Head to west	Undeterminable	Left side	Right side	Face down	Face up	Undeterminable	Flexed, left side	Flexed, right side	Semiflexed, left side	Semiflexed, right side	Extended, on back	Undeterminable			
1			x					x				x						?	Al
2	x							x						x			x	♀	Al
3	x							x						x			x	♀	Et
4				x		x							x				x	♀	Ad
5	x					x								x			x	♂	30–35
6					?					?				x			x	?	Ad
8				?						?	x						x	♂	30–35
9	x								x					x			x	♂	35–40
10	?									x					x			♀	Al
11	x					x					x						x	♂	35–40
12			x							x						x	x	?	I
13			x				x									x		?	I
14			x				x									x		♂	Al
15	x						x						x				x	♀	Lt
16			x					x								x		?	I
17			x				x									x	x	♂	30–35
18			x						x							x	x	?	I
19				x		x						x					x	♀	Al
20					?					x			x					♀ ?	Ad
21			x							x						x	x	?	Ad
22			x							x						x	x	♀ ?	Ad
23	x					x						x						♂	Al
24		x				x							x				x	♀	40+
Totals	8	1	3	3	8	6	4	4	2	7	2	3	4	5	1	8	16	23	

[1] (I=infant; Al=adolescent; Ad=adult; Lt=late teens; Et=early teens)

nent teeth except three adolescents, who showed only slight tooth wear. It is assumed that the wear was produced by the gritty particles unintentionally added to the staple food, cornmeal, when it was being ground on sandstone metates.

Caries and abscesses are fairly common in Mesa Verde burials, but they were observed only in Burial 9 at Big Juniper House. There is no explanation for this rarity.

The poor condition of most of the bones may have been due to the shallowness of the trash mound. Disturbance of many of the burials was probably caused by rodents and badgers burrowing into the deposits.

Following are descriptions of the 23 burials:

Burial 1 (fig. 165, center)

Location—Test Trench 1, South Trash Mound.
Sex—Indeterminate.
Age—Adolescent.
Condition—Badly disturbed and fragmentary; trunk, arms, and hands and feet missing.
Deformation—Pronounced asymmetrical lambdoidal deformation.
Pathology—None.
Position—Head partly on right side, face-down. Leg bones suggest a flexed burial on the right side.
Associated artifacts—None.
Comments—No evidence of excavated grave. Base of skull 1.3 feet below surface and 0.6 foot above sterile earth.

Burial 2 (fig. 165, right)

Location—Test Trench 1, South Trash Mound; same general location as Burial 1.
Sex—Female.
Age—Adolescent.
Condition—Humeri, left ulna, and hands and feet missing.
Deformation—Pronounced asymmetrical lambdoidal deformation.
Pathology—None.
Position—Semiflexed; head face-down; trunk is breast-down, legs flexed on right side, left leg over right; knees at about right angles to the trunk; arms probably extended on both sides of the trunk.
Associated artifacts—Turkey bone tubular bead near right side of radius of right arm; one Type 3 worked sherd of Mancos Black-on-white in area of burial.
Comments—No evidence of excavated grave. Burial is 1.6 feet below surface, and rested on sterile soil. All deciduous teeth present and heavily worn; no permanent teeth have erupted.

Burial 3 (fig. 165, left)

Location—Test Trench 1, South Trash Mound, same general location as Burials 1 and 2.
Sex—Female.
Age—Early teens.
Condition—Left forearm, and hands and feet missing.
Deformation—Moderate asymmetrical lambdoidal deformation.
Pathology—50° bilateral anteversion of the femora.

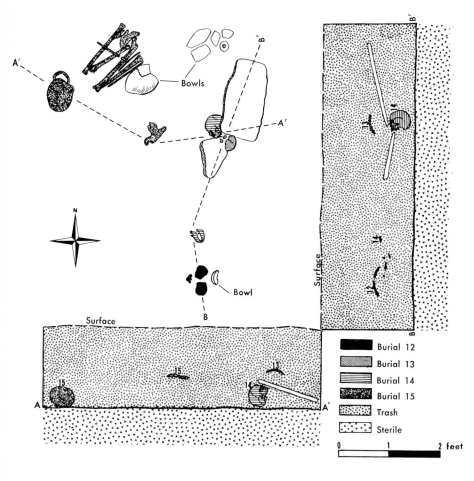

173 *Burials 12, 13, 14, and 15, Test Trench 8, South Trash Mound.*

Burial 14 (fig. 173)

Location—Test Trench 8, South Trash Mound—same area as Burials 12, 13, and 15.

Sex—Male.

Age—Adolescent.

Condition—Only skull and mandible present.

Deformation—Pronounced asymmetrical lambdoidal deformation.

Pathology—None.

Position—Skull was on the right side and facing slightly upward; mandible, southwest of skull, inverted.

Associated artifacts—None.

Comments—No grave observed. Two unworked, rectangular slabs had been placed around the skull: the larger one, 1.7 feet long by 1.5 feet wide by 0.3 foot thick, covered the left side of the skull; and the smaller slab, 1.1 feet long by 0.7 foot wide by 0.3 foot thick, was placed next to the right side of the skull. Cranial capacity is 1,110 cc. Only permanent teeth erupted were the maxillary central incisors; no tooth loss, caries, or abscesses. Burrows in the area suggest rodents removed or contributed to destruction of other bones of this burial.

Burial 15 (fig. 173)

Location—Test Trench 8, South Trash Mound, areas of Burials 12, 13, and 14.

Sex—Female.

Age—Late teens.

Condition—Trunk and arms missing.

Deformation—Pronounced asymmetrical lambdoidal deformation.

Pathology—None observed.

Position—Skull to southwest, on right side; legs flexed on right side with left leg slightly over right leg at ankle area and left knee to the east of the right knee. Not possible to determine degree of flexion due to missing bones, but probably a tightly flexed burial.

Associated artifacts—About half of a Mancos Black-

174 *Burials 16 and 17, Test Trench 11, South Trash Mound. Arrows point to scattered remains of Burial 16.*

174

175   *Burial 18, Test Trench 8, South Trash Mound.*

on-white bowl (fig. 56d) next to lower left tibia and
fibula; about a third of a large Mancos Black-on-white
bowl (fig. 56e) to the east of the first.

Comments—No grave observed. Burial resting on
sterile soil, 1.1 feet below surface. Rodent burrows in the
area suggest probable reason for fragmentary remains.
All permanent dentition had erupted except third molars;
no tooth loss; no caries or abscesses; and little tooth wear.

Burial 16 (fig. 174)

Location—Test Trench 11, South Trash Mound.
Sex—Indeterminate.
Age—Infant.
Condition—Disturbed and fragmentary; skull missing.
Deformation—No data.
Pathology—Not possible to determine due to fragmentary remains.
Position—Not observable because bones were not in
articulated position.
Associated artifacts—None.
Comments—No evidence of prepared grave. Burial,
0.3 foot above sterile soil and 0.5 foot below surface, may
have been a secondary one.

Burial 17 (fig. 174)

Location—Test Trench 11, South Trash Mound, next
to Burial 16.
Sex—Male.
Age—30 to 35.
Condition—Elements scattered.
Deformation—Pronounced asymmetrical lambdoidal
deformation.

Pathology—Arthritis of the vertebrae, elbow, and
glenoid; 30° exterior torsion of tibia.
Position—Not determinable. Skull on right side, facing slightly upward; mandible to right of skull, inverted.
Associated artifacts—A fragmentary Bluff-La Plata
Black-on-red Type 6 worked sherd in skull area.
Comments—No grave observed. Top of skull 0.5 foot
below surface and bottom of skull 0.2 foot above sterile
soil. Tooth loss: all permanent dentition erupted; antemortem loss of all mandibular teeth with exception of
both canines and left first premolar; loss of maxillary
dentition with exception of right central incisor, premolars 1, canines, molars 1 and 2. No caries or abscesses;
teeth heavily worn. Cranial capacity is 1,320 cc. Stature
estimated (from tibia) at 166.7 cm., or about 5 feet
4 inches.

Burial 18 (fig. 175)

Location—Test Trench 8, South Trash Mound.
Sex—Indeterminate.
Age—Infant.
Condition—Fragmentary.
Deformation—Pronounced asymmetrical lambdoidal
deformation.
Pathology—None.
Position—Not possible to determine due to partial remains; skull face-up and turned slightly to one side.
Associated artifacts—About half of a McElmo Blackon-white bowl (fig. 73b) next to the left side of the skull.
Comments—No evidence of prepared grave; top of
skull 1 foot below surface; bottom of skull 0.2 foot above
sterile soil.

176 *Burials 19 and 20, Test Trench 11, South Trash Mound. Pitcher at left associated with Burial 19.*

177 *Burial 22, Kiva A.*

Burial 19 (fig. 176)

Location—Test Trench 11, South Trash Mound.
Sex—Female.
Age—Adolescent.
Condition—Arms, hands and feet missing.
Deformation—Pronounced asymmetrical lambdoidal deformation.
Pathology—None observed.
Position—Flexed, face-down; legs flexed on right side, left leg over right and knees drawn up to the chest area.
Associated artifacts—Mancos Black-on-white pitcher (fig. 58d) at left shoulder; one corrugated jar body sherd and one Mancos Black-on-white bowl body sherd next to left hip (table 3).
Comments—No grave observed. Top of skull 1 foot below surface; burial resting on and slightly in the sterile earth. No permanent dentition; all deciduous dentition present except second molars.

Burial 20 (fig. 176)

Location—Test Trench 11, South Trash Mound, area of Burial 19.
Sex—Probably female.
Age—Adult.
Condition—Scattered; skull missing.
Deformation—No data.
Pathology—None.
Position—Probably semiflexed on right side, with knees at right angles to trunk.
Associated artifacts—None.
Comments—No grave observed. Top of right ilium 0.1 foot below surface; burial 0.7 foot above sterile soil and 0.4 foot above Burial 19.

Burial 21

Location—Test Trench 14, South Trash Mound. This burial represents two individuals; the more complete one is detailed below.
Sex—Indeterminate.
Age—Adult.
Condition—Fragmentary and scattered; skull missing.

176

Deformation—No data.
Pathology—None.
Position—Not determinable.
Associated artifacts—Probably a rectangular red shale pendant (fig. 133c) found in the burial area.
Comments—No grave observed; bones near the surface. The second burial is represented only by the skull. Sex is indeterminate, age is adolescent; pronounced asymmetrical lambdoidal deformation; all deciduous dentition erupted except the second molars; no caries or abscesses, and no tooth wear (incisors missing). Skull was 3 feet from the first burial; it was 0.7 foot below the surface and rested on sterile soil. There were no associated artifacts; no evidence of a prepared grave was found.

Burial 22 (fig. 177)

Location—Kiva A, Level 6 (bottom), near ventilator shaft.
Sex—Probably female.
Age—Adult.
Condition—Fragmentary and scattered.
Deformation—No data.
Pathology—The distal portion of the right humerus shows perforation of the olecranon fossa.
Position—Not determinable.
Associated artifacts—Possibly a restorable Mancos Black-on-white jar (fig. 57b), the sherds of which were scattered on the floor and around the ventilator shaft, near the burial.
Comments—No excavated grave. Burial 2.2 feet below top of banquette and 1 foot above the floor of the kiva. Fragments of a skull (adult, of indeterminate sex) were below rest of bones and may represent another burial.

The existence of other scattered human bones, numerous sherds, and miscellaneous trash in the lower fill of Kiva A suggests the kiva was used as a dump and perhaps also as a convenient burying place.

Burial 23 (fig. 178)

Location—Test Trench 14, South Trash Mound.
Sex—Male.
Age—Adolescent.
Condition—Left side of skull missing.
Deformation—Pronounced asymmetrical lambdoidal deformation.
Pathology—Acetabular arthritis.
Position—Semiflexed, on left side; head partially face-down; arms tightly flexed, with elbows next to chest; right arm flexed over left; legs flexed with knees at about right angles to the trunk, right leg over left.
Associated artifacts—None.
Comments—No evidence of grave; burial near surface. All deciduous dentition erupted, no permanent tooth eruption; no tooth wear.

Burial 24 (fig. 179)

Location—Bottom of Cist 2, Room 18.
Sex—Female.
Age—Over 40.
Condition—Nearly complete except for most of arms.
Deformation—Pronounced asymmetrical lambdoidal deformation.
Pathology—Moderate acetabular arthritis.
Position—Semiflexed, on left side; head on left side; trunk on left side and curved; right arm over left, probably flexed; legs flexed on left side, right leg over left; knees at about right angles to the trunk; elbows may have been at knees.
Associated artifacts—Partially restorable Mancos Corrugated jar next to pelvis; sherds and stone artifacts in the fill (tables 3 and 9) possibly associated.

178 *Burial 23, Test Trench 14, South Trash Mound*

Comments—Burial rested on floor of cist, 4.7 feet below surface. Most of dentition lost; oldest individual found at site. The cist was probably used originally for storage.

179 *Burial 24, at bottom of Cist 2, Room 18.*

summary and conclusions

Big Juniper House was occupied primarily in late Pueblo II and early Pueblo III. There is some evidence that the site was also inhabited intermittently, or by a small group of people, in early Pueblo II.

Components A and B, the first occupations of the site, are represented by only a few structures, possibly built by one or two families. The two components may be parts of a single component, assignable to the latter half of the 10th century.

The next occupation, Component C, dates from the 1050's to about 1080. The number and kinds of architectural features, which include Kiva A, suggest a population of 20 to 30 individuals. Jacal structures are the most notable features of this component.

Component D, dating from about 1080–1100 to 1130, comprises the most extensive remains at Big Juniper House. The three kivas and nearly all the surface masonry rooms are associated with this component. The population probably numbered between 50 and 75 people. During this occupation, changes from the Pueblo II to the Pueblo III pattern occurred.

Component E, dating from about 1130 to 1150, is represented by the "later walls" built over Kivas A and B by the compound wall north of Rooms 5 and 24. It is possible that Component D rooms remained in use during this terminal occupation. If such was the case, the population may have remained relatively constant. The peculiar "later walls" are featured at other sites on Wetherill Mesa. They may have had some ceremonial purpose.

Trade or contact with areas outside of the Mesa Verde area is indicated by the presence of obsidian artifacts, foreign pottery, and the killed-bowl burial. Obsidian was probably obtained from New Mexico or the San Juan Mountains near Pagosa Springs, Colorado. Puerco and Wingate Black-on-red pottery came from the upper Little Colorado drainage and Tusayan Polychrome pottery from the Kayenta area in northeastern Arizona and southeastern Utah. The killed-bowl burial suggests culture con-

tact with the Mimbres area of southwestern New Mexico. Generally speaking, contact with regions outside the Mesa Verde seems to have been slight.

The excavation of Big Juniper House is of importance mainly for the information it provided regarding the transitional stage from Pueblo II to Pueblo III in the Mesa Verde area. This stage is represented in Components D and E and dates between A.D. 1080 and 1150. Certain traits were introduced during this stage, and some of these were apparently limited to it (see table 16).

TABLE 16.—TRAITS MARKING THE PUEBLO II–PUEBLO III TRANSITION

TRAITS	Introduced during this period	Most common in this period	Limited to this period
Architecture:			
Double walls	x		
Pecked-faced masonry	x		
Kivas integrated with rooms	x		
Later walls over kivas		x?	
Flared pilasters	x		
Set-back pilasters	x		
Southern recess	x		
Liner above banquette	x		
Six-pilaster kiva	x?		
Ceramics:			
Mummy Lake Gray		x	
Mesa Verde Corrugated	x		
Early McElmo Black-on-white	x	x	x
Stone Artifacts:			
Plain/troughed metate	x	x	x
Plain-faced metate	x		
Type 2 mano	x	x	x
Bone Artifacts:			
Humerus scraper	x		

ARCHITECTURE

The integration of kivas with surface rooms begins during the transitional stage or shortly earlier. This relationship is shown most clearly at Big Juniper House in the placement of Kiva B, the kiva with probably the latest construction date at the site. The detached position of Kiva A exemplifies the older, "pure" Pueblo II layout.

The kivas of Big Juniper House have two features indicative of the transition: (1) six pilasters that are flared and set back from the edge of the banquette, and (2) a liner above the banquette. Another transitional feature of kivas, not found at Big Juniper House, is the southern recess, the deepened interpilaster space in the southern part of the banquette over the ventilator tunnel.

Walls over kivas, double-wall construction, and pecked-face masonry undoubtedly appear first during the transitional stage. Double walls and pecked-face masonry seem to be most common in late Pueblo III.

CERAMICS

Several features of the ceramics of Big Juniper House are indicative of the transition from Pueblo II to Pueblo III. The early style McElmo Black-on-white was introduced at this time. On present evidence, this pottery seems to be limited to this stage, and to be superseded after 1150 by other styles of McElmo, or "proto-Mesa Verde Black-on-white," and by "classic" Mesa Verde Black-on-white. The absence of the latter two kinds of pottery is important negative evidence for the Pueblo II–III transition.

The increasing use of carbon paint on Mancos Black-on-white is indicative of the change to the Pueblo III habit. The evidence indicates that Mancos Black-on-white, still the dominant decorated pottery type of the transitional stage, declined after 1150.

In the realm of utility pottery, Mummy Lake Gray reached the zenith of its popularity during this time. Mesa Verde Corrugated began to be made, but Mancos Corrugated was the principal corrugated type until about 1150. The greater percentage of flaring rims, as opposed to straight rims, on Mancos Corrugated pottery may be an indicator of the change to Pueblo III style of sharply everted rims on Mesa Verde Corrugated.

STONE ARTIFACTS

Two stone artifact types appear to be limited to the Pueblo II–III transition: the plain/troughed metate and the Type 2 mano. Perhaps these should be regarded not as new types but as older types remodeled to fit the new grinding pattern.

Plain-faced metates also originated during the Pueblo II–III transition and were the dominant type in Pueblo III. Although no manos made specifically for use with these metates were found at Big Juniper House, they were probably introduced during this stage.

BONE ARTIFACTS

The humerus scraper, represented by only one fragment at Big Juniper House, is a common type in Pueblo III components in the Mesa Verde area and may have been made initially during the transitional stage. Comparative studies now under way may disclose that other types of bone artifacts are definitely associated with cultural stages in this area.

Artifacts and refuse from sites in the Mesa Verde show that turkeys became increasingly important as time passed. It is evident, from the findings at Big Juniper House, that mammals were still preferred during the transition to Pueblo III, and also that the more equal utilization of mammals and birds (mainly turkeys) did not occur until after A.D. 1150.

references

ABEL, LELAND, J.
1955. Pottery Types of the Southwest, Harold S. Colton, ed. Museum of Northern Arizona Ceramics Series, no. 3. Northern Arizona Society of Science and Art. Flagstaff.

BREW, JOHN OTIS
1946. Archaeology of Alkali Ridge, Southeastern Utah. Papers of the Peabody Museum of American Archaeology and Ethnology, Harvard University, vol. 21. Cambridge.

BURKITT, MILES
1963. The Old Stone Age: A Study of Palaeolithic Times. Atheneum, New York.

CARLSON, ROY L.
MS. White Mountain Red Ware: A Stylistic Tradition in the Prehistoric Pottery of East Central Arizona. Unpublished Ph. D. dissertation, 1961. University of Arizona. Tucson.

COLTON, HAROLD S.
1956. Pottery Types of the Southwest, Harold S. Colton, ed. Museum of Northern Arizona Ceramics Series, no. 3C. Northern Arizona Society of Science and Art. Flagstaff.

COSGROVE, H. S. and C. B.
1932. The Swarts Ruin, A Typical Mimbres Site in Southwestern New Mexico. Papers of the Peabody Museum of American Archaeology and Ethnology, Harvard University, vol. 15, no. 1. Cambridge.

CUTLER, HUGH C., and WINTON MEYER
1965. Corn and Cucurbits from Wetherill Mesa. Memoirs of the Society for American Archaeology, no. 19; American Antiquity, vol. 31, no. 2, pt. 2, pp. 136–152. Salt Lake City.

ERDMAN, JAMES A.
MS. Ecology of the Pinyon-Juniper Woodland of Wetherill Mesa, Mesa Verde National Park, Colorado. Unpublished M.A. thesis, 1962. University of Colorado. Boulder.

FEWKES, JESSE WALTER
1910. Cremation in Cliff-dwellings, Colorado and Arizona. Records of the Past, vol. 9, pt. 3, pp. 154–156. Washington.
1911. Antiquities of the Mesa Verde National Park: Cliff Palace. Bureau of American Ethnology, bulletin 51. Washington.

GUTHE, C. E.
1925. Pueblo Pottery Making, A Study at the Village of San Ildefonso. Papers of the Phillips Academy, Southwestern Expedition, no. 2. New Haven.

HAYES, ALDEN C.
1964. The Archeological Survey of Wetherill Mesa, Mesa Verde National Park, Colorado. Archeological Research Series 7-A. National Park Service. Washington.

HODGE, FREDERICK W.
1920. Hawikuh Bonework. Indian Notes and Monographs, vol. 3, no. 3, pp. 61-151. Museum of the American Indian, Heye Foundation. New York.

JUDD, NEIL M.
1954. The Material Culture of Pueblo Bonito. Smithsonian Miscellaneous Collections, vol. 124. Washington.

KIDDER, ALFRED VINCENT
1932. The Artifacts of Pecos. Papers of the Phillips Academy, Southwestern Expedition, no. 6. New Haven.

LANCASTER, JAMES A., and JEAN M. PINKLEY
1954. Excavation at Site 16 of Three Pueblo II Mesa-Top Ruins, in Archeological Excavations in Mesa Verde National Park, Colorado, 1950. Archeological Research Series 2. National Park Service. Washington.

MANG, FRED E., JR.
1965. The View Camera in Archaeological Photography. Memoirs of the Society for American Archaeology, no. 19; American Antiquity, vol. 31, no. 2, pt. 2, pp. 227–230. Salt Lake City.

MORRIS, EARL H.
1919. The Aztec Ruin. Anthropological Papers of the American Museum of Natural History, vol. 26, pt. 1, pp. 1–108. New York.
1924. Burials in the Aztec Ruin. Anthropological Papers of the American Museum of Natural History, vol. 26, pt. 3, pp. 139–225. New York.
1939. Archaeological Studies in the La Plata District. Carnegie Institution of Washington, publication 519. Washington.

MORRIS, EARL H., and ROBERT F. BURGH
1954. Basketmaker II Sites near Durango, Colorado.

Carnegie Institution of Washington, publication 604. Washington.

NORDENSKIÖLD, GUSTAF
1893. The Cliff Dwellers of the Mesa Verde, Southwestern Colorado; Their Pottery and Implements (English trans. by D. Lloyd Morgan). P.A. Norstedt and Soner. Stockholm and Chicago.

O'BRYAN, DERIC
1950. Excavations in Mesa Verde National Park, 1947–1948. Medallion Papers, no. 39. Gila Pueblo. Globe, Ariz.

OSBORNE, CAROLYN M.
1965. The Preparation of Yucca Fibers: An Experimental Study. Memoirs of the Society for American Archaeology, no. 19; American Antiquity, vol. 31, no. 2, pt. 2, pp. 45–50. Salt Lake City.

OSBORNE, DOUGLAS
1965. Chipping Remains as an Indication of Cultural Change at Wetherill Mesa. Memoirs of the Society for American Archaeology, no. 19; American Antiquity, vol. 31, no. 2, pt. 2, pp. 30–44. Salt Lake City.

PARSONS, ELSIE CLEWS
1939. Pueblo Indian Religion. The University of Chicago Press. Chicago.

REED, ERIK K.
1958. Excavations in Mancos Canyon, Colorado. University of Utah, Anthropological Papers, no. 35. Salt Lake City.

ROBERTS, FRANK H. H., JR.
1932. The Village of the Great Kivas on the Zuñi Reservation, New Mexico. Bureau of American Ethnology, bulletin 111. Washington.

ROHN, ARTHUR H.
1959. A Tentative Classification of the Pottery from the Mesa Verde Region. Mimeographed. Mesa Verde National Park, Colo.

1965. Postulation of Socio-economic Groups from Archaeological Evidence. Memoirs of the Society for American Archaeology, No. 19; American Antiquity, vol. 31, no. 2, pt. 2, pp. 65–69. Salt Lake City.

ROHN, ARTHUR H., and JERVIS D. SWANNACK, JR.
1965. Mummy Lake Gray: A New Pottery Type. Memoirs of the Society for American Archaeology, no. 19; American Antiquity, vol. 31, no. 2, pt. 2, pp. 14–18. Salt Lake City.

WANEK, ALEXANDER A.
1959. Geology and Fuel Resources of the Mesa Verde Area, Montezuma and La Plata Counties, Colorado. Geological Survey, bulletin 1072–M. Washington.

WHEELER, RICHARD P.
1965. Edge-abraded Flakes, Blades, and Cores in the Puebloan Tool Assemblage. Memoirs of the Society for American Archaeology, no. 19; American Antiquity, vol. 31, no. 2, pt. 2, pp. 19–29. Salt Lake City.

WOODBURY, RICHARD B.
1954. Prehistoric Stone Implements of Northeastern Arizona. Papers of the Peabody Museum of American Archaeology and Ethnology, Harvard University, vol. 34. Cambridge.

appendix

TABLE 17.—TREE-RING DATES FROM BIG JUNIPER HOUSE[1]

Specimen [2]	Provenience	Dates, A.D.[3] Inside	Dates, A.D.[3] Outside	Specimen [2]	Provenience	Dates, A.D.[3] Inside	Dates, A.D.[3] Outside
MV-1637	Room 1b, lower fill	915	1008vv	MV-1692	Kiva B, floor fill	927	1130B
MV-1640	Room 1a, lower fill	908p	1006vv	MV-1694	Room 8, subfloor fill	925	990vv
MV-1642	Room 1a, lower fill	828p	1027vv	MV-1695	Room 8, subfloor post	873	1000vv
MV-1645	Room 1a, lower fill	652	750+vv	MV-1700	Room 1a, Floor 2, Post 1	837±	1031r
MV-1646	Room 1a, lower fill	791	1017vv	MV-1701	Room 1a, Floor 2, Post 2	710	1039vv
MV-1649	Room 1a, lower fill	777±	1045vv	MV-1702	Room 1a, Floor 2, Post 3	832p	971vv
MV-1650	Room 1a, lower fill	803	1054vv	MV-1703	Room 1a, lower fill	790	945vv
MV-1651	Room 1a, lower fill	886	1035vv	MV-1704	Room 1a, lower fill	824	890vv
MV-1653	Room 1a, lower fill	755	1052vv	MV-1705	Room 1a, lower fill	886	1031vv
MV-1655	Room 7, subfloor fill	824	1025vv	MV-1707	Room 1a, Floor 2, jacal wall, Post 3	876	990vv
MV-1659	Kiva B, Level 3	823	1048vv	MV-1709	Room 1a, Floor 2, jacal wall, Post 5	875	974vv
MV-1660	Room 10, lower fill	893±	1007vv	MV-1710	Room 1a, Floor 2, jacal wall, Post 2	669	773v
MV-1666	Room 10, lower fill	879p	985r	MV-1712	Room 1a, Floor 2, jacal wall, Post 7	877	949vv
MV-1667	Room 10, lower fill	931p	1022+vv	MV-1713	Room 1a, Floor 2, jacal wall, Post 8	636	770vv
MV-1668	Room 10, lower fill	921	1039vv	MV-1715	Room 1a, lower fill	637	774vv
MV-1670	Room 10, lower fill	925	1027vv	MV-1716	Room 1a, lower fill	933	990vv
MV-1672	Room 10, lower fill	859p	947vv	MV-1718	Room 19, fill	782	891+vv
MV-1673	Room 10, lower fill	933p	1028vv	MV-1725	Room 7, subfloor cist, Post 1	886	983+vv
MV-1677	Room 10, lower fill	924	992vv	MV-1726	Room 7, subfloor cist, Post 2	827	988+vv
MV-1678	Room 10, lower fill	910	1018vv	MV-1730	Room 7, subfloor cist fill	928	992vv
MV-1679	Room 10, lower fill	814	886vv	MV-1732	Room 7, subfloor, Post 2	914p	1021vv
MV-1680	Room 10, lower fill	893	1041vv	MV-1733	Room 19, subfloor cist fill	908	977vv
MV-1685	Room 10, lower fill	800	1008+vv	MV-1735	Room 10, Floor 2, Cist 1 fill	911	1024vv
MV-1686	Room 10, Floor 2, Post 1	855±	993vv	MV-2133	Room 1b, lower fill	915p	952vv
MV-1687	Room 10, Floor 2, Post 2	812p	1028+vv	MV-2138	Room 5, Cist 1 fill	990p	1047vv
MV-1688	Kiva B, Level 3	897	1062+vv				

[1] All dates listed derive from juniper charcoal or charred wood (*Juniperus*).
[2] Specimen numbers assigned by Laboratory of Tree-Ring Research, University of Arizona.
[3] Key to symbols: p—pith ring present; v—outside shows erosion, outermost ring variable around circumference; vv—outside shows extreme erosion, outermost rings very variable; r—outer ring constant over significant portion of circumference; B—bark present on outside.

index

A

Abajo Red-on-orange: 63, 96–98
Abel, Leland J.: 64, 65, 72–74, 78, 88, 97
abrading stones: 55, 124–126
Alkali Ridge: 63, 96
Anasazi: 51
anvil: 53, 139
Awatovi Expedition: 119
awls: 147–153
axes: 55, 126, 130, 131, 133
Aztec Ruin: 169, 171

B

Badger House: 17, 74, 78, 79, 105, 107, 118
Basketmaker III: 64, 73, 109, 171
beads: 53, 139, 155, 167, 171
bitted stones: 133
Bluff Black-on-red: 96, 98
bone artifacts:
    awls: 147–153
    bodkin: 147
    cache or tool kit: 55, 150, 151, 154
    knifelike object: 154
    knives (or scrapers) : 60
    ornaments:
        beads: 155, 167
        performated mammal tibias: 154, 155
    problematical objects: 156
    scrapers: 55, 153, 154, 180
    tool blank: 155
    tool kit or cache: 55, 150, 151, 154
Brew, John Otis: 96, 97
Burgh, Robert F., and Earl H. Morris: 134
burials:
    burned: 38, 53, 171
    cist: 45, 177
    cremation: 171
    killed-bowl: 166, 168, 169, 179
    pathologies: 165–167, 171–173, 175, 177
    positions, defined: 166
    teeth: abscesses, caries, loss, wear: 166, 167
Burkitt, Miles: 135

C

Carlson, Roy L.: 99
ceremonial object: 53, 139, 140
Chapin:
    Black-on-white: 63, 64, 73
    Gray: 63, 64
chipping debris: 60, 159
choppers: 133
cists (pits, storage jars) : 28, 35–38, 40, 41, 44–48, 50, 52, 53, 55, 59, 107 177
Citadel Polychrome: 63
Cliff Palace: 171
Colton, Harold S.: 64, 99
concretions: 53, 55, 59, 60, 142, 144
cores, utilized: 138
corn: 161
Cortez Black-on-white: 33, 36, 47, 49, 53, 60, 63, 73–75, 78, 79, 86, 91, 94, 99, 103–107, 169, 173
Cosgrove, H. S. and C. B.: 169
crushers: 46, 122, 123
Cutler, Hugh C., and Winton Meyer: 161

D

drills: 135

E

Erdman, James A.: 19

F

Fewkes, Jesse Walter: 139, 171

unclassified corugated: 67, 100, 105, 107, 176
University of Arizona: 20
University of Pennsylvania Museum: 103

V

Village of the Great Kivas: 139

W

Wanek, Alexander A.: 18
Wheat, Joe Ben: 74
Wheeler, Richard P.: 136
whetstone: 124
Wetherill Black-on-white: 94
Wingate Black-on-red: 99, 179
Woodbury, Richard B.: 109, 115, 119, 120, 124, 129

Y

Yellow Jacket district: 74, 93

U.S. GOVERNMENT PRINTING OFFICE: 1970 O - 243-356